DISEASES & DISORDERS

Fetal Alcohol Syndrome

Gail B. Stewart

LUCENT BOOKS

A part of Gale, Cengage Learning

GALE
CENGAGE Learning

Detroit • New York • San Francisco • New Haven, Conn • Waterville, Maine • London

GALE
CENGAGE Learning·

LIBRARY OF CONGRESS CATALOGING-IN-PUBLICATION DATA

Stewart, Gail B. (Gail Barbara), 1949-
  Fetal alcohol syndrome / by Gail B. Stewart.
    p. cm. -- (Diseases and disorders)
  Includes bibliographical references and index.
  ISBN 978-1-4205-0695-2 (hardcover)
  1. Fetal alcohol syndrome. 2. Children of prenatal alcohol abuse.
I. Title.
  RG629.F45S74 2012
  618.3'26861--dc23

                                            2011047288

Lucent Books
27500 Drake Rd.
Farmington Hills, MI 48331

ISBN-13: 978-1-4205-0695-2
ISBN-10: 1-4205-0695-1

Printed in the United States of America
1 2 3 4 5 6 7 16 15 14 13 12

Table of Contents

"The Most Difficult Puzzles Ever Devised"

Charles Best, one of the pioneers in the search for a cure for diabetes, once explained what it is about medical research that intrigued him so. "It's not just the gratification of knowing one is helping people," he confided, "although that probably is a more heroic and selfless motivation. Those feelings may enter in, but truly, what I find best is the feeling of going toe to toe with nature, of trying to solve the most difficult puzzles ever devised. The answers are there somewhere, those keys that will solve the puzzle and make the patient well. But how will those keys be found?"

Since the dawn of civilization, nothing has so puzzled people—and often frightened them, as well—as the onset of illness in a body or mind that had seemed healthy before. A seizure, the inability of a heart to pump, the sudden deterioration of muscle tone in a small child—being unable to reverse such conditions or even to understand why they occur was unspeakably frustrating to healers. Even before there were names for such conditions, even before they were understood at all, each was a reminder of how complex the human body was, and how vulnerable.

While our grappling with understanding diseases has been frustrating at times, it has also provided some of humankind's most heroic accomplishments. Alexander Fleming's accidental discovery in 1928 of a mold that could be turned into penicillin has resulted in the saving of untold millions of lives. The isolation of the enzyme insulin has reversed what was once a death sentence for anyone with diabetes. There have been great strides in combating conditions for which there is not yet a cure, too. Medicines can help AIDS patients live longer, diagnostic tools such as mammography and ultrasounds can help doctors find tumors while they are treatable, and laser surgery techniques have made the most intricate, minute operations routine.

This "toe-to-toe" competition with diseases and disorders is even more remarkable when seen in a historical continuum. An astonishing amount of progress has been made in a very short time. Just two hundred years ago, the existence of germs as a cause of some diseases was unknown. In fact, it was less than 150 years ago that a British surgeon named Joseph Lister had difficulty persuading his fellow doctors that washing their hands before delivering a baby might increase the chances of a healthy delivery (especially if they had just attended to a diseased patient)!

Each book in Lucent's Diseases and Disorders series explores a disease or disorder and the knowledge that has been accumulated (or discarded) by doctors through the years. Each book also examines the tools used for pinpointing a diagnosis, as well as the various means that are used to treat or cure a disease. Finally, new ideas are presented—techniques or medicines that may be on the horizon.

Frustration and disappointment are still part of medicine, for not every disease or condition can be cured or prevented. But the limitations of knowledge are being pushed outward constantly; the "most difficult puzzles ever devised" are finding challengers every day.

INTRODUCTION

"The World Seems to Move So Fast"

Joyce (her last name is withheld at her request) apologizes for being late. She has just come home from doing an errand, and she did not think it would take this long. She pauses and then clarifies what she has been doing. "I'm late because I was up at my grandson's school. Fourth time this week, and it's only Thursday," she says. "[My husband] David and I try to take turns doing this stuff, but he's out of town today and tomorrow, so it's me. All me."[1]

Joyce is young for a grandmother—just forty-seven—but jokes that on many days she feels twice that age. She and David have been legal guardians of their seven-year-old grandson Chase since December 2004, when the boy was just six months old. "I preface this by saying that we absolutely adore Chase," she says. "I'm glad we've got him. But honestly? The last thing we thought we'd be doing now would be raising a grandchild, especially one like our little guy, who has so many special needs."[2]

Born and Diagnosed

Chase was born with fetal alcohol syndrome (FAS), a disease that can occur in an unborn baby when the pregnant mother drinks alcohol. It can cause brain damage, resulting in mental retardation, as well as a range of physical problems. Chase's biological mother, Joyce and David's daughter Tina, is an alcoholic. Because of her addiction, she was unable to stay completely sober during her pregnancy. As a result of her drinking, Chase was affected by the alcohol in her system.

Chase was diagnosed with FAS almost immediately after his birth. One doctor told Tina that because of FAS, her son would face a number of challenges in his life—behavioral and physical, as well as likely mental retardation and other disabilities that would make it more difficult for him to learn. Aware that she was not stable enough to raise a child—especially one with so many health issues—Tina turned to her parents for help.

"Tina had been in and out of treatment for several years since she was fifteen," says Joyce, noting that

> I think she really has tried very hard, but she has not had much success with it. So when she asked us to take Chase, we said yes—of course we did. What could we have said? He's family. He's ours. He has so many problems, so many problems that he deals with—how could we let him be put into foster care or the adoption system? I could never live with myself, and David feels the same way. But yes, it is far, far more challenging than anything we've ever done. And to be honest, it's getting harder all the time.[3]

A Range of Problems

Though Chase is only seven, the disease is already making his life difficult in a number of ways. "He's very small for his age—he looks like one of the kindergarteners," Joyce says, adding,

> He has asthma and has serious vision problems. His pediatrician recently detected a heart murmur. And more and more, he just sort of tunes out—he just seems to be in a world by himself. Although his teacher couldn't be nicer, I know it is difficult for her. He doesn't fit in, he doesn't pay attention. She's got a room full of first-graders, and she can't spend the whole time taking care of Chase.[4]

Infants with fetal alcohol syndrome have been exposed to heavy levels of alcohol in the womb when their mothers drank alcohol during pregancy. The alcohol damages the fetal brain and results in mental retardation and physiological problems.

Joyce explains that Chase disappeared from his class today—which explains why she was called up to his school. "He has started wandering out the door of the classroom when [the teacher] turns her head, and that's what today's emergency was all about," Joyce explains. "After almost fifteen minutes, she found him down by the maintenance room—in the hall, just sitting by himself on the floor playing with a rubber band he'd found."[5]

"The World Seems to Move So Fast"

Joyce says that she is relieved that he was unharmed, but she knows the bigger problem has not been solved. "I know this is a really hard situation. It's hard for Chase, because he doesn't understand why people were upset, and it's hard for the teacher, because she shouldn't have to take so much time away from the other kids to track him down all the time. And it's not like we have a special school we could send him to—there just isn't a school for children like him anywhere close."[6]

She knows that Chase's whole life is going to be a difficult struggle, for his problems will only increase. "David and I are trying as hard as we can, and there are some very good days. He can be the sweetest boy in the world. But the thing is, Chase is starting life with a lot more going against him than the average kid does. He's not only got serious health issues, but with his mental disabilities, things are just so hard, and we know they'll keep getting harder. The world seems to move so fast, and Chase just can't keep up."[7]

CHAPTER ONE

The Evolution of a Disease

Every year in the United States, forty thousand babies are diagnosed with one of a range of birth defects that are caused by prenatal (before birth) exposure to alcohol. The most severe of these is fetal alcohol syndrome, or FAS. According to some medical researchers, however, there are many more babies whose alcohol-related birth defects go undiagnosed, often because these defects are not immediately recognizable to doctors when the baby is born and because the effects can be misdiagnosed as other disorders. As a result, researchers suspect that the number of children affected by their mothers' drinking alcohol while pregnant is actually much higher than statistics indicate.

Fetal alcohol syndrome (FAS) and other alcohol-related birth abnormalities account for more birth defects than other common causes, including Down syndrome, spina bifida, and muscular dystrophy. And what makes the prevalence of FAS so tragic is that unlike these other diseases, FAS is actually preventable. Some say it is 100 percent preventable.

An Ancient Suspicion

Fetal alcohol syndrome was not identified as a medical issue until the 1960s; however, dating back even to ancient times, there have been people who suspected that by drinking alcohol, a pregnant woman might be damaging her unborn child. They did not have any scientific data to support their suspicions, however; merely observations and anecdotal evidence.

For example, in 330 B.C., the Greek philosopher Aristotle noted, "Foolish, drunken and hare-brained women most often bring forth children like unto themselves, morose and languid."[8] In ancient Sparta and Carthage, there was a custom that prevented newlyweds from drinking any alcoholic beverage on their wedding night, lest any child conceived might be damaged.

In 330 B.C. the Greek philosopher Aristotle noted that "Foolish, drunken and hare-brained women most often bring forth children like unto themselves, morose and languid." His observations are thought to be the first description of FAS.

In the late seventeenth and early eighteenth centuries, some European scientists observed that women who drank alcohol while pregnant seemed more likely to suffer miscarriages or stillbirths or to have sickly, underweight children. In 1726, British doctors speculated that alcohol might be dangerous to unborn babies, and as a result, too many youngsters were destined to become a drain on society. In a special report to Parliament in 1726 the Royal College of Physicians wrote that parental drinking "is too often the cause of weak, feeble, and distempered children, who must be, instead of an advantage and strength, a charge to their country."[9]

"Unhappy Influence"

Stephen Hales was an Anglican priest and early researcher of alcohol's effects on unborn children. Though he had no science to back up his ideas, his descriptions sound very much like twenty-first-century descriptions of babies born with FASD.

Nay, the unhappy influence of these liquors reaches much farther than to the destruction of those who indulge in the use of them . . . [and includes] the children that are yet unborn. Of this we have too frequent instances, where the unhappy mothers habituate themselves to these distilled liquors, whose children, when first born, are often either of a diminutive, pigmy size, or look withered and old, as if they had numbered many years, when they have not, as yet, alas! attained to the evening of the first day. How many more instances are there of children, who tho' born with good constitutions have unhappily sucked in the deadly spirituous poison with their nurses' milk. . . .

Missing the Connection

But while such observations noted a connection between alcohol and unhealthy babies, few believed that the alcohol itself was directly affecting the fetus. Instead, they believed, health problems of these babies were not caused by alcohol, but by the poverty, bad hygiene, and poor eating habits of mothers who were drinkers. In fact, some scientists even suggested that since most of these women were "lower class" or "undesirable," the alcohol was acting as a selective poison, weeding out the weaker, less desirable members of society.

Whence it is evident that in proportion as the contagion spreads farther and farther among mankind, so must the breed of human species be proportionately more and more depraved, and will accordingly degenerate more and more from the manly and robust constitution of preceding generations.

English physiologist Stephen Hales (1677–1761) was an Anglican priest and early researcher of alcohol's effect on unborn children.

Quoted in David F. Musto. *Drugs in America: A Documentary History.* New York: New York University Press, 2002, p. 21.

By the 1950s, in many countries throughout the world—including the United States—drinking by pregnant women was on the rise. Doctors did not perceive a connection between prenatal alcohol consumption and birth defects. Some distinguished writers and scholars dismissed the notion that alcohol could do any harm to the unborn baby. For example, in his 1964 best-selling book *Life Before Birth*, noted British anthropologist Ashley Montagu argued that there was absolutely

In his 1964 book, *Life Before Birth*, Ashley Montagu (pictured) postulated that a mother's alcohol consumption had no effect on her unborn fetus. Four years later Paul Lemoine would disprove Montagu's findings and be the first to describe what would later be known as FAS.

nothing to worry about, no matter how much alcohol a pregnant woman were to drink:

> Unexpectedly, alcohol in the form of beverages, even in immoderate amounts, has no apparent effect on a child before birth. . . . It can now be stated categorically . . . that no matter how great the amounts of alcohol taken by the mother—or the father, for that matter—neither the germ cells nor the development of the child will be affected. . . . An amount of alcohol in the blood that would kill the mother is not enough even to irritate the tissues of the child.[10]

The Discovery of a Disease

In 1968, four years after the release of *Life Before Birth*, Dr. Paul Lemoine, a pediatrician in Nantes, France, published a scholarly paper that contradicted Montagu's view that alcohol use by a pregnant woman was harmless to the fetus. Lemoine was the first to describe what would later be known as fetal alcohol syndrome. He worked in a home for infants and young children whose mothers could not care for them. Lemoine noticed that many of the children born to alcoholic mothers seemed to share certain facial deformities, defects of the central nervous system, and unusually stunted growth.

With the help of his medical colleagues, Lemoine wrote a paper describing 127 of these children and suggesting that these effects were the result of prenatal alcohol exposure. He submitted the paper to a prestigious French medical journal, but it was rejected. Instead, he published the data in a small regional journal, which did not circulate internationally. As a result, his work went unnoticed.

Five years later, however, in 1973, another article about the effects of alcohol on the unborn appeared in the prestigious British medical journal the *Lancet*. This article documented the work of a group of scientists headed by Dr. David Smith and Dr. Kenneth Jones from the University of Washington. They studied infants born to alcoholic mothers at Harborview Hospital in Seattle.

Dr. David Smith, pictured, along with Dr. Kenneth Jones of the University of Washington studied infants born to alcoholic mothers. They noted that the babies failed to gain weight, were uninterested in nursing, and frequently cried. They were the first to name the syndrome, fetal alcohol syndrome, and to describe the symptoms.

Besides noting a range of physical deformities in the infants, Smith and Jones described the babies' failure to gain weight, their apparent lack of interest in nursing, and their poor sucking ability, as well as how infrequently they cried for attention. The doctors engaged the assistance of a child psychologist, who discovered that the infants had varying degrees of brain damage. Finally, Smith and Jones gave this collection of symptoms its name: fetal alcohol syndrome.

Unlike the work of Lemoine, the article by Smith and Jones received a great deal of international attention. Research groups were formed in a number of countries to study alcohol and its effects on their populations. Scientists were interested in testing the findings of the Smith and Jones's study and to know whether fetal alcohol syndrome was more common within certain groups within a population. They were also interested in studying the long-range effects of prenatal alcohol exposure, how much exposure would put the fetus at risk, and whether there might be a cure for FAS or therapies that might help such children. The questions about this new disease seemed endless.

Three Criteria for an FAS Diagnosis

Early research by Smith, Jones, and other medical experts helped identify the physical symptoms of the disease, some of which are noticeable at birth while others are only evident as the child grows.

The first physical sign is low birth-weight and a slow pattern of growth in the child. Babies born with FAS are found to be at or below the tenth percentile for height, weight, or both. The second is damage to the central nervous system (CNS), which may or may not be apparent in a newborn child. CNS damage can give infants poor muscle tone, an inability to nurse, or a smaller-than-average head size. An unusually small head, a condition known as microcephaly, often indicates a problem with brain development and can lead to mental retardation or other learning problems that will be more noticeable as the child grows.

A third physical sign of FAS is the presence of specific facial abnormalities. These include a very thin upper lip, a flattened face, and a smaller-than-average lower jaw. Babies with FAS have smaller-than-average mouths and lack a noticeable philtrum, the vertical groove between the nose and upper lip. Their eyes tend to be wide set, with smaller eye openings. Sometimes babies with FAS have a short, upturned nose, and their ears are set lower on the head.

Ann Streissguth, a psychiatrist and one of the pioneers in the study of FAS, recalls doing a psychological assessment in January 1973 of seven young children that Smith and Jones had identified as having fetal alcohol syndrome. She saw that these children clearly had brain damage that was apparent by their erratic, jerky movements and poor coordination. Streissguth remembers thinking later that although the children represented three racial groups and were not at all related, their similarity to one another was almost eerie.

The first physical sign of FAS is a low birth-weight and a slow pattern of growth in the child.

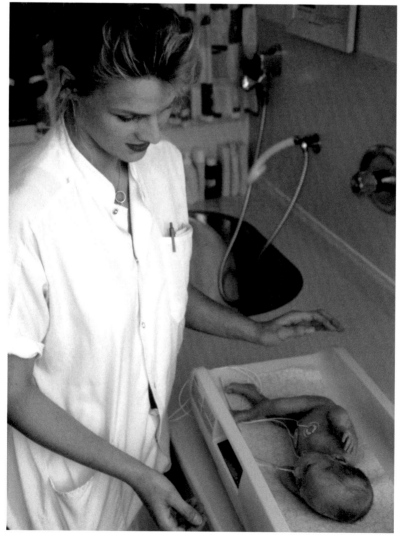

[They had] small, sparkly eyes; small heads; and an appearance about the mouth that appeared as though they were pursing their lips even when they weren't smiling. Except for the two who were still infants and the one who was so flaccid [limp] she was carried in the arms of her mother, the other children had a wispy, flighty quality. I thought to myself that these children who were so curiously and surprisingly unafraid of me were like butterflies.[11]

Partial Fetal Alcohol Syndrome (PFAS)

As more and more research was done on fetal alcohol syndrome, however, scientists began to realize that some children whose mothers had a confirmed history of drinking while pregnant had only some of the signs of FAS. For example, some children displayed the same damage to their central nervous systems as those with FAS, yet they lacked the obvious facial abnormalities that had become an identifiable aspect of FAS.

By the early twenty-first century researchers understood that the effects of alcohol on a developing fetus could take other forms besides full-blown FAS.

Doctors began diagnosing children with partial fetal alcohol syndrome, or PFAS. Children with PFAS have only mild facial abnormalities or none at all. As with children with FAS, these children are often in the lowest percentiles for weight and height and have damage to their central nervous systems.

Six-year-old Lily, from Winnipeg, Canada, received her diagnosis of PFAS in June 2010. She is very small for her age, and like many children who have prenatal alcohol exposure, her eyesight is poor. Her face has what her adoptive mother, Janice, calls

a "pancake" look. That's the best way I can describe it. It's flatter than what you see in other kids her age. It's especially noticeable around her eyes. That's the alcohol damage, the doctors say. But really, that's the only unusual thing you'd notice physically about Lily—if you even noticed it at all—besides her being very petite. We don't know how much Lily's birth mother drank, but we do know that she has a history of drinking.[12]

A Related Disorder

Another group of FAS cases includes children who may exhibit no outward physical abnormalities that are present in children with FAS but still have damage to their central nervous systems caused by their mothers' drinking. These children are not mentally retarded, nor are they smaller than average. But their prenatal exposure to alcohol has resulted in a range of other problems that may include difficulty paying attention or remembering, poor impulse control, or a lack of social skills. This condition is known as Alcohol-Related Neurodevelopmental Disorder, or ARND.

That is the case with Davy, a boy who was adopted at the age of two by a Wisconsin couple, Roger and Darla. Darla says that they had no idea that he might suffer from the effects of prenatal alcohol exposure until Davy's birth father wrote them a letter through the adoption agency. In the letter he explained that Davy's birth mother was an alcoholic and had drunk alcohol throughout her pregnancy.

Even so, Darla says, she and her husband would never have guessed, since Davy never exhibited any of the physical signs of FAS.

> We never knew that [Davy] had birth defects from alcohol. I've seen pictures of babies and little kids with fetal alcohol syndrome, you know, and [Davy] doesn't look like them. He's not retarded, either. But he's always had a *lot* of school problems—and a lot of social problems, too. . . . Most of his teachers have said at one time or another that he lacks impulse control. He gets very angry and upset when he isn't able do something, gets very impatient. A short fuse, my husband calls it. He's a good kid, but he definitely has challenges that make his life tougher.[13]

The Umbrella of FASD

Most doctors today use the umbrella term *Fetal Alcohol Spectrum Disorders* (FASD) to include FAS, PFAS, and ARND. FASD is not a diagnosis, but the term is used to describe the wide range of effects that can occur in a child whose mother

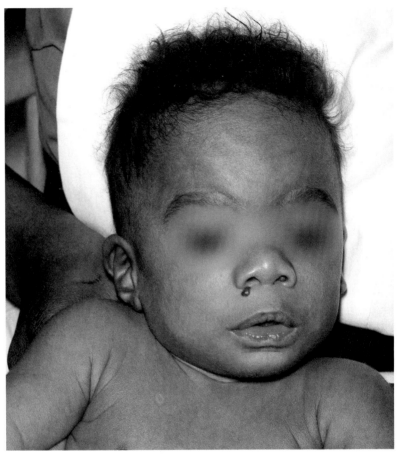

This four-month-old baby born was born with fetal alcohol syndrome. Though some children may not show the mental and physical defects of FAS, they often experience other problems related to it.

drank alcohol during her pregnancy. It is important, say doctors, that people understand that there is a spectrum of symptoms of prenatal alcohol damage.

"You meet a lot of people who assume that just because a baby doesn't have the face you think of with fetal alcohol syndrome—the wide-set eyes or the smooth area between the nose and upper lip—that child is free of damage," says Bill, a South Dakota father whose adopted daughter has been diagnosed with ARND, adding, "and that's not so."[14]

He says that he can see why experts say that full-blown FAS is only the tip of a large iceberg.

[FAS is] a terrible disease, and there are a lot of very nasty physical problems that often go with it. [My wife and I] have met people whose FAS-afflicted children are living with very severe heart problems, for example. . . . But in some ways, kids who have the ARND and partial FAS, they maybe have less in terms of physical disabilities, but they can make up for that by having the behavioral issues, the problems with memory, with balance, with handling school. I keep telling people that [FASD] really *is* like an iceberg, because there's some pretty dangerous stuff you *can't* see when they're babies.[15]

"It's Not an Absolute Scale"

One of the puzzles about prenatal alcohol exposure is that not all pregnant women who drink will deliver a baby with FAS or FASD. Scientists are not yet certain why some pregnant women who drink during their pregnancies deliver normal, healthy babies while others deliver babies with severe symptoms of FAS. Researchers think that the amount of alcohol a woman drinks, and when she drinks it, are important factors, but even when these factors are the same, the effect on the fetus can differ. The rate of affected babies born to alcoholic mothers is between 40 and 50 percent. Some studies suggest that it is just as dangerous for a pregnant woman to have a drink every day during her pregnancy as it is for a pregnant woman to binge-drink; that is, to have several drinks in a very short time, such as at a celebration or party.

Dr. Sterling Clarren, one of the world's foremost authorities on FAS and FASD, says that even though not every pregnant woman who drinks will give birth to a baby with the disease, he believes drinking alcohol during pregnancy is very, very risky. "It's sort of like drunk driving," he explains. "It's not an absolute scale, it's a relative scale. The more you drink and then drive, the higher your risk of having an accident. But of course, many people, I guess luckily, get drunk, get behind the

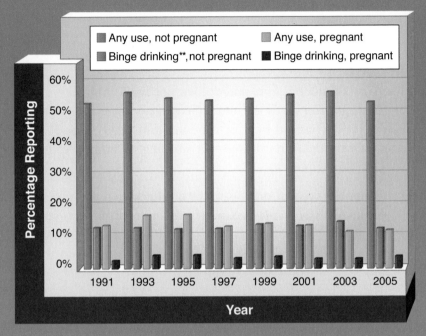

Alcohol Use Among Women Aged 18–44, 1991–2005*

Legend:
- Any use, not pregnant
- Any use, pregnant
- Binge drinking**, not pregnant
- Binge drinking, pregnant

Y-axis: Percentage Reporting (0% – 60%)

X-axis: Year (1991, 1993, 1995, 1997, 1999, 2001, 2003, 2005)

*Behavioral Risk Factor Surveillance System (BRFSS) surveys, United States
**Binge drinking is defined as having five or more drinks on at least one occasion in the past 30 days.

Taken from: Centers for Disease Control and Prevention. www.cdc.gov/ncbddd/fasd/data.html.

wheel and get home safely. But the more you drink, the higher your risk; the less you drink, the lower your risk."[16]

Clarren says that though there are standards for testing the amount of liquor one can put into one's bloodstream before driving, no such standards exist for how much a pregnant woman can drink without harming her unborn baby.

At some point, the state has put a line in the sand and said, "Above this line of alcohol in your blood it's illegal for you to drive a car." But people below that line on a dark night in an unusual circumstance might still be impaired. It's the same thing. Women who drink voluminously, who get drunk, who binge drink, place their fetuses at significant risk. But there are fetuses who get through that OK. Women who drink less put their babies at less risk; but they never put their babies at zero risk.[17]

Alcohol Is Alcohol

The type of alcohol consumed does not make a difference in the damage it does to the fetus. Women who drink so-called lighter drinks such as beer or wine are taking the same risk as women who drink hard liquor, according to counselor Mary Werner. She explains:

> It's not the type of drink—that's a fallacy that some people have. They think that maybe instead of having hard liquor, like whiskey or vodka or gin, they'll be safe by having beer. That's completely wrong. It has to do with the amount of liquor that is contained in that drink. A bottle of beer, a 5-ounce glass of wine, and a shot of liquor—that's 1.5 ounces [of alcohol]—these are all classified as a drink. So I tell clients, don't be fooled by pretty packaging. Wine coolers, hard lemonade—you drink enough of those, you might as well be drinking shots [of hard alcohol]. Your unborn baby won't know the difference.[18]

Who Is at Risk?

Race, ethnicity, and economic status make absolutely no difference in assessing which babies are more likely to be affected by alcohol exposure. It is true, however, that the behaviors that cause prenatal alcohol effects are more likely to occur among groups in which heavy drinking or alcoholism is a bigger problem. In the United States, fetal alcohol exposure tends to be more common in babies born to poor or uneducated women. Also, teenagers tend to be more inclined to drink when pregnant.

Some of the highest percentages of babies with FAS or FASD occur in certain Native American communities, where unemployment, poverty levels, and alcoholism are often much

The type of alcohol consumed does not make a difference in the damage it does to a fetus. Women who drink lighter alcoholic drinks, such as beer or wine, still run the same risk as those who consume hard liquor.

more prevalent than the national average. In 2007, the Centers for Disease Control and Prevention showed that the FAS rate among Indians is thirty times higher than among whites. "I would say it's very definitely a problem, almost pervasive," says Sandra Parsons, director of family and children's services for the Red Lake Band of Ojibwa in northern Minnesota. "I haven't found anybody yet who disputes that. I think people would literally be amazed at how prevalent [it is.]"[19]

All Around the World

The United States is not the only nation experiencing a problem with FAS and FASD. There are places throughout the world where the numbers of people with prenatal alcohol damage are troubling, too. Canada's First Nation (Indian) people have many of the same problems as American Indians—poverty, unemployment, hopelessness, and alcoholism. As a result, the number of victims has reached epidemic proportions. In 2008, it was estimated that nearly one in five babies born to First Nation mothers showed the effects of FAS.

South Africa, too, has a severe FAS problem. In fact in the southern part of the country, as many as 10 percent of babies

State-Specific Weighted Prevalence Estimates of Alcohol Use (Percentage of Any Use/Binge Drinking) Among Women Aged 18–44 Years — BRFSS, 2008

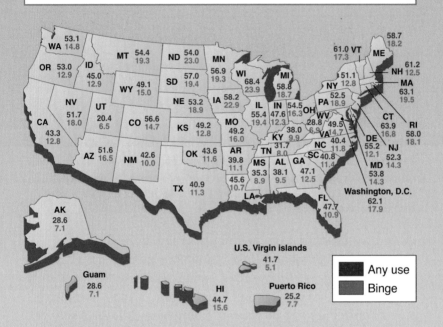

State	Any use	Binge
WA	53.1	14.8
OR	53.0	12.9
ID	45.0	12.9
MT	54.4	19.3
ND	54.0	23.0
MN	56.9	19.3
WI	68.4	23.9
MI	58.8	18.7
VT	61.0	17.3
ME	58.7	18.2
NH	61.2	12.5
NV	51.7	18.0
UT	20.4	6.5
WY	49.1	15.0
SD	57.0	19.4
NE	53.2	18.9
IA	58.2	22.9
IL	55.4	19.4
IN	47.6	12.3
OH	54.5	16.3
PA	52.5	18.9
NY	51.1	12.8
MA	63.1	19.5
CA	43.3	12.8
CO	56.6	14.7
KS	49.2	12.8
MO	49.2	16.0
KY	38.0	9.9
WV	28.8	6.9
VA	49.5	14.7
CT	63.9	16.8
RI	58.0	18.1
AZ	51.6	16.5
NM	42.6	10.0
OK	43.6	11.6
AR	39.8	11.1
TN	31.7	8.0
NC	40.4	11.8
SC	40.8	11.4
DE	55.2	12.1
NJ	52.3	14.3
MD	53.8	14.3
TX	40.9	11.3
MS	35.3	8.9
AL	38.1	9.5
GA	47.1	12.5
LA	45.6	10.7
FL	47.7	10.9
Washington, D.C.	62.1	17.9
AK	28.6	7.1
Guam	28.6	7.1
HI	44.7	15.6
U.S. Virgin islands	41.7	5.1
Puerto Rico	25.2	7.7

Legend: ■ Any use   ■ Binge

- 12.2 percent of pregnant women (about one in eight) reported any alcohol use in the past thirty days. This rate has remained stable over the fifteen-year period.
- Pregnant women most likely to report any alcohol use were:
  - Thirty-five to forty-four years of age (17.7 percent)
  - College graduates (14.4 percent)
  - Employed (13.7 percent)
  - Unmarried (13.4 percent)
- 1.9 percent of pregnant women (about one in fifty) reported binge drinking in the past thirty days.*
  - Pregnant women who binge drank were more likely to be employed and unmarried as compared with pregnant women who did not binge drink.
  - The prevalence of binge drinking among pregnant women did not substantially change over the fifteen-year period.
- Alcohol use levels prior to pregnancy are a strong predictor of alcohol use during pregnancy.
  - Many women who drink alcohol continue to drink during the early weeks of pregnancy because they do not realize that they are pregnant.
  - Only about 40 percent of women realize that they are pregnant at four weeks of gestation, a critical period for organ development.

are born with FAS. For many years, black workers in white-owned vineyards were paid by the tot system; that is, they were given a flask of wine (known as a "tot") for their work instead of a monetary wage. Though the tot system was outlawed in 1961, the effects of alcoholism among the population—including many pregnant women—continue to the present day. According to the World Health Association, 1 million South Africans have full-blown FAS, while another 5 million have FASD.

A Daily Struggle

For children born with the disease, life is often a day-by-day, even minute-by-minute, struggle. There are physical ailments that are often part of the disease—poor eyesight, heart problems, hearing and breathing problems, and slack muscles. But there are also a range of behavioral issues that can be just as debilitating, such as low self-esteem, a lack of impulse control, poor memory, and inadequate social skills.

But the difficulties are also shared by the parents—whether biological or adoptive—who love them, who want to see their children lead full, happy lives but are confronted by the limitations of FAS and FASD every day. Marsha, a Michigan woman whose nine-year-old adopted daughter, Carly, has FAS, says that the biggest challenge is to stay positive. "Every morning I wake up thinking that it's a new day, lots of possibilities, you know? By lunchtime, though, it seems like I'm struggling to stay optimistic."[20]

The hardest thing, she says, is the inevitable comparison between Carly and other children her age.

> Carly has so many great qualities, but she has such trouble. She can't remember things she seemed to know backwards and forwards ten minutes before. She is disorganized—can't hang on to her backpack or school stuff. But the worst is that she hasn't found a friend yet. And that tears me up inside. You know, when your child is [an infant], you imagine her having birthday parties, playing dolls out in the yard with her friends, or riding bikes. But that's not going to happen for Carly—at least I can't see it ever happening.[21]

CHAPTER TWO

Alcohol's Effects on the Fetus

David Smith and Kenneth Jones learned in their early research that prenatal exposure to alcohol can cause birth defects. This resulted in alcohol being classified as a teratogen. From the Greek word meaning "monster maker," a teratogen is any substance that can harm the healthy growth of a fetus as it develops in its mother's womb and cause birth defects.

There are other dangerous teratogens besides alcohol, including natural elements like mercury, certain ingredients in pesticides, and many different medications. For example, in the late 1950s many doctors prescribed a drug called thalidomide to pregnant women because it relieved the unpleasant symptoms of morning sickness. Scientists later found that the drug was harmful to unborn babies. Thousands of babies born to women who had taken thalidomide had severe deformities, including missing or flipper-like arms and legs. The drug was taken off the market in 1961.

After thalidomide was banned, health officials began to look much more closely at other drugs or substances that might be used by pregnant women, so that further tragedies could be avoided. Says medical technician Aisha Charya,

It's happened with a whole lot of prescription drugs. Things are tested much more vigorously [today]. Even medicines that can be lifesaving to certain people could be dangerous to a fetus, and as soon as a substance is found to be [a teratogen], the public gets warned. I mean, how many times do you hear on TV ads these days, such and such a pill "should not be used by women who are pregnant or who could become pregnant." It means that the drug is a teratogen.[22]

Studying Teratogens

Figuring out which substances are teratogens is only one aspect of a drug researchers' job. They also work to figure out how the toxins cause damage, what amount is harmful to the fetus, and whether the timing of the exposure is a factor. For example, exposure to a substance may pose a danger to the fetus while certain organs are developing. Months later, when the organs have developed, that substance may not be harmful.

Researchers were eager to learn more about how alcohol causes damage to a fetus and what types of damage it could do.

In the early 1960s doctors prescribed the drug thalidomide to pregnant women. As a result, thousands of deformed babies were born to these women.

They wanted to know how much alcohol a pregnant woman could drink before it posed a danger to her baby; whether alcohol had effects other than those noted in Smith and Jones's 1973 study; whether the fetus was more at risk during certain periods of the pregnancy; and what the long-term effects of prenatal alcohol exposure might be.

Since that first study, researchers throughout the world have conducted hundreds of experiments using laboratory animals. They studied how alcohol affects the bodies of adult rats, monkeys, dogs, and sheep, as well as observing alcohol's effects on their unborn fetuses. Scientists noted not only physical effects but also psychological and emotional ones. The experiments have enabled them to understand how alcohol can cause such extensive damage to a developing human fetus.

How Alcohol Affects an Unborn Baby

Everything a pregnant woman drinks or eats affects her unborn baby because their bodies are interconnected. The fetus lives within the placenta, an organ that is attached to the mother's uterus. Until the baby is born, everything necessary for its development and growth comes to it by way of the placenta.

When a pregnant woman drinks, the blood vessels in her stomach absorb the alcohol and transmit it directly into her bloodstream. The alcohol remains in the bloodstream until it is metabolized, or broken down, by various chemicals in the body—especially in the liver. Meanwhile, the alcohol in the mother's system passes easily from her bloodstream to the placenta, where it directly affects the fetus.

Scientists say that the level of alcohol in the fetus rises far above that of the mother. That's because as an adult, the mother has a number of bodily systems that process alcohol; however, for the fetus, depending on how much it has developed, these systems may not exist or they may be immature and process the alcohol much more slowly. For example, the liver of an unborn baby, which develops during the first four weeks of pregnancy, can do less than 10 percent of the job of an adult's liver.

When a pregnant woman drinks, the blood vessels in her stomach absorb the alcohol, and it passes easily from her bloodstream to the placenta, where it directly affects the fetus.

To make things even worse, the fluid within the placenta that cushions the fetus acts like a reservoir tank, holding the toxic alcohol for many hours a time. This means that the fluid inside the placenta actually has a higher alcohol level than the mother's bloodstream. Michael Dorris, an adoptive father of a child with FAS writes, "The baby in the womb becomes more drunk than the mother with every drink of liquor, wine, or beer she takes. By the time she feels tipsy . . . the child she carries could, in effect, have already passed out."[23]

The Damage Alcohol Does

Once the fetus is exposed to alcohol, the damage begins. The alcohol dehydrates the delicate cells of the developing fetus, disrupting and slowing their growth. In some cases the cells can get so dehydrated that they die. Scientists observed this cell damage, along with other effects, when they gave alcohol regularly to pregnant rats. When the rat litters were born, many of them had malformed legs, toes, eyes, ears, and internal organs. Many of them had smaller heads than normal, too. Such deformities were far more common than in the offspring of rats who had not been given alcohol.

Researchers were surprised to find that in some cases severe birth defects occurred even when the rats had been given alcohol only on one or two days of their pregnancies. For instance, rats that had been given two "binge" doses of alcohol on day seven of their pregnancy gave birth to baby rats with facial abnormalities that were very much like those of young children with FAS. The baby rats had smaller-than-normal heads and narrower foreheads. They also had thin upper lips and smaller-than-normal eye openings.

In other experiments, researchers were able to use those findings to discover when the facial characteristics of FAS typically occur in human pregnancies. According to FAS expert Sterling Clarren, some of the facial abnormalities that are the physical signs of FAS only occur when a pregnant woman drinks on certain days early in her pregnancy—unfortunately, at a time when many women do not even yet realize that they are pregnant.

"A couple of those facial features do seem to be very point specific and occur in humans on the 19th or 20th day of pregnancy," Clarren explains. "So if you don't drink exactly at that time, you won't get some of the facial features, and if you don't get some of the facial features, people don't get to the final diagnosis of fetal alcohol syndrome."[24]

The Effects of Alcohol on Brain Development

While the facial abnormalities occur only when a pregnant woman drinks on certain days, the brain damage that occurs with FAS and FASD can occur throughout a pregnancy, from the very beginning to the end. In its mother's uterus, a developing fetus grows 150 million brain cells each day. Such damage or loss is usually irreversible.

That damage and loss of brain cells was clearly visible when researchers performed autopsies on some of the rats with FAS.

The brain damage that is done by alcohol can occur throughout pregnancy. In the mother's uterus a developing fetus can have its brain development severely curtailed.

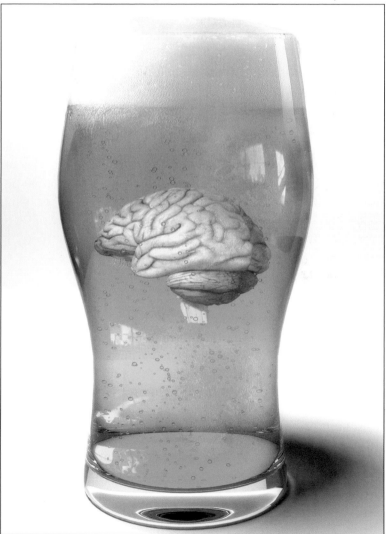

Their brains were much smaller than the brains of normal rats. Certain parts of the brain were malformed or in some cases missing altogether. These brain abnormalities occur in the brains of babies born with FAS, too. Some of these result in a limited ability of the child to remember and learn, to control impulsive behavior, and to use good judgment. Frequently this damage also affects the hypothalamus, that part of the brain that controls emotions, hunger and thirst, temperature, and pain sensation.

Researchers have again turned to animal experiments to understand how the loss of critical brain cells due to alcohol damage might affect humans with FAS. In one experiment researchers gave a task to baby chicks that were exposed to alcohol before they hatched. The researchers wanted to see how quickly those baby chicks could learn a task, compared with normal chicks. They placed the chicks in a pen with a bowl of food. They placed a piece of clear plastic in front of the food so, to reach it, the chicks needed to back up and go around that small barrier. While the normal chicks had no trouble figuring this out, the FAS chicks had difficulties even after being shown the correct way to the food several times. Many of them continued to walk into the plastic over and over, not learning from their mistakes.

Brain Development and Behavioral Problems

In addition to causing learning difficulties, brain damage from prenatal alcohol exposure can cause a number of behavioral problems, including impulsiveness and short attention span. Kateanne Ryan, a kindergarten teacher for twelve years in Alberta, Canada, says that she has taught several children who were later diagnosed with FAS or FASD.

> Most of the children [had] what we determined was ADD [attention-deficit disorder]. They seemed to have so much trouble staying on task, even if it was just for ten minutes, when we were coloring or something like that. I've had a few who absolutely could not settle at all. They couldn't

Children with FAS or FASD have difficulty concentrating and staying on task, much like children who suffer from ADD (attention-deficit disorder). Many children originally diagnosed with ADD have been found to have FAS.

concentrate; they couldn't listen. They'd just get up and start moving around the room. I remember one little girl would see a picture one of the other kids was coloring and she'd pick it up and wouldn't give it back. And she had no idea why the child who colored the picture was sad or mad. She just liked the picture and wanted to take it home. She didn't think of it as stealing or anything like that.[25]

Ryan says that at the time, most of those children had not yet been diagnosed with FASD. "When we [teachers] found out," she says, "we were not at all surprised. It made perfect sense when you read the literature about FAS and FASD. The more you learn about prenatal alcohol exposure and what it can do, the more you realize how extensive the brain damage associated with it can be. It wasn't misbehavior. It was just the way their brains worked."[26]

An International Issue

The growing numbers of FAS children has become an international issue because of the increased numbers of American families adopting babies from Russia, a country with one of the highest rates of FAS in its orphanages. As with a number of other adoptive parents, Chip and Julie Harshaws of Virginia learned that their adopted Russian child, Roman, had FAS after noticing disturbing behavior, as related in the following excerpt.

> Life in the Harshaw household became a grim slide from normalcy as his parents and siblings tried to cope with Roman's volatile behavior.
>
> One day, Roman and Grace were playing in the backyard when Grace grew tired of the game and began to walk away. Roman, suddenly enraged, picked up a 2-by-4. Only his mother's scream stopped him from smashing his sister in the head.
>
> "Two minutes later, he had no idea what he'd done," Julie Harshaw said.
>
> Another time, a family friend was watching the children when Roman pulled Grace into the backyard pool and held

A Difficult Diagnosis

Even with so many behavioral and physical markers that have been noted by FAS researchers, it is sometimes difficult for doctors to diagnose, especially in infants. Diagnosis is easier when the doctor knows the mother drank alcohol during her pregnancy and the physical symptoms are obvious. But the characteristic facial features of FAS can be subtle and difficult to spot in a newborn. Other physical problems or brain damage may not be immediately evident. Also, no single symptom definitively shows the presence of FAS, and many symptoms her underwater until the friend jumped in, fully clothed, and pulled her out. He has also tried to attack his sister with a steak knife.

Once he tied a kite string around his neck and the top of a slide, then slid down, snapping the string and cutting a bloody ring around his neck. He has gouged three teeth out of his mouth with items like a spoon and a pen cap.

Trying to correct his behavior is futile, his parents say, because he doesn't understand consequences. Time outs in his room don't work—he escapes through the window. The Harshaws installed an alarm system in their home, not to keep burglars out but to keep Roman in. . . .

They say that when they aired their grievances to [the adoption agency], the agency's proposed solution was to dissolve the adoption and take Roman back—an outcome that they say they would never consider.

"This isn't a dog in a kennel," Chip Harshaw said.

"We love him to death," Julie Harshaw said. "He's our son."

Bill Sizemore. "Good Intentions Pave a Hard Road." *Norfolk Virginian-Pilot*, April 22, 2010, p. 1.

of FAS can be attributed to other causes. There is no blood test, brain scan, or X-ray that will confirm that a baby has the disorder. Instead, doctors have to make what is called a clinical diagnosis by observing a combination of physical features, organ defects, and/or central nervous system damage and then determining as best they can the mother's health and habits during pregnancy—and that can be extremely difficult.

Even experts in FAS can struggle to make a definitive diagnosis in babies and young children. For example, one physical characteristic common in FAS is smaller-than-usual eyes.

Researchers provide ranges that suggest whether the eye measurement is normal or might indicate an FAS deformity, but getting the precise measurement of a baby's or young child's eye opening can be tricky. As Clarren explains, even a slight error can make all the difference in a diagnosis. "It is very difficult to measure the size of [an eye opening] especially if [the patient isn't] looking at you," he says.

> You are holding a ruler in front of somebody's face and you have to do that with an accuracy of one millimeter. If you are off by one millimeter, you could be off by a standard deviation. If people have epicanthal folds [folds of skin of the upper eyelid seen in Asian and some Native American babies] or any other soft tissue around their eyes, you have to pull that away so that you can accurately measure this . . . and you have to do that in a flying three-year old.[27]

Verifying that the mother did indeed use alcohol during her pregnancy can also be very difficult. Now that the effects of alcohol on unborn babies are well known and pregnant women are warned against using alcohol, women who continue to drink during their pregnancies are more likely to be ashamed or embarrassed to admit to it. And that can make the diagnosing of FASD that much harder.

That is what Jennifer Poss Taylor, a Texas mother, learned when she and her husband adopted Ashley. Besides being extremely small for her age, the nineteen-month-old had facial features that made Taylor wonder if she might have FAS. "I was concerned because of her distorted features," writes Taylor, "a wide spread between her eyes, and a flatter than normal upper lip—all of which are indicators of FAS."[28]

Predictable Denial

Taylor and her husband requested that Child Protective Services investigate whether Ashley's birth mother drank alcohol during the pregnancy. The "investigation" was merely a quick phone call to ask the woman if she had ever drunk alcohol while pregnant. The answer was no, and though Ashley was

Studies have shown the main reason women drink during pregnancy is due to domestic violence.

diagnosed with FAS years later, many experts say the birth mother's denial was predictable.

"It is common to deny doing something like this. No one wants to admit to it," says social worker Mary Werner, who has worked with many at-risk families where alcoholism is a problem. "To them, it's akin to someone asking them if they beat their children. But you have to understand that many of these women are living in abusive relationships, in poverty, in situations where drug and alcohol use is an everyday thing."[29]

There is little disagreement that alcohol abuse is often a response to very difficult life situations. Clarren did a research project at the University of Washington on the backgrounds of the surviving mothers of 162 children with FAS (about 25 percent of the mothers were either missing or dead). In his study, which included women of a range of ethnic and educational backgrounds, he found that 100 percent had been seriously abused either by parents when they were children, by husbands or boyfriends as adults, or by both. Having experienced such abusive relationships, Clarren explains, it is not surprising that these women used alcohol to cope. "It was a universal experience," he says. "The sexual abuse stories were so horrible that the nurse who did these interviews . . . needed therapy herself after she completed [them]."[30]

Werner has worked with clients who tried very hard to limit their drinking once they learned they were pregnant. "There are so many variables there," she says.

> Some of them found out they were pregnant after they'd been partying pretty hard on the weekends, and all of sudden they find out they're pregnant. Then they get scared about what was going to happen. Was the baby going to die? Would it be deformed? Would the baby be taken away from her? And, by the way, that's what often happens with babies born to alcoholic mothers. They're put into foster care. So, no, it is not surprising in the least [that] some mothers absolutely deny drinking."[31]

Diagnosing FASD

As hard as it is to diagnose full-blown FAS—even when a doctor is looking for it—it is far more difficult to detect the presence of the other disorders on the FAS spectrum because the physical effects are more subtle. Facial abnormalities—if they exist at all—can be so mild that they are overlooked. The brain damage, which is part of all disorders on the FAS spectrum, is not always visible or measurable in a young child. In fact, most of the FASD diagnoses occur after a child has begun school.

But while diagnosis is difficult, it certainly is not impossible, according to M.J. Hofer, diagnostic specialist for the Minnesota Organization on Fetal Alcohol Syndrome (MOFAS). "We find that a team approach works best," she says. "As that child grows, more symptoms can become more apparent. We use a range of professionals, from pediatricians to MDs, from psychologists and psychiatrists to speech therapists."[32]

They may spot signs of trouble; for example, the child who has been in four or five foster homes. They look for children with central nervous system damage that has resulted in limitations of what are known as the "executive functions" of the brain. "Those are the children who just don't seem to get it," says Hofer. "They have difficulty organizing themselves, a hard time self-regulating rather than having to be told constantly what they should be doing, for example. They have so much trouble understanding the idea of actions and consequences."[33]

Much of her work, says Hofer, is systematically eliminating other conditions that could cause such problems. "It's rule out, rule out, rule out," she says. "You ask, can this be autism? Is it ADD or some other disorder? You go through any other condition that may cause similar symptoms. You just keep looking."[34] Eventually the team can get to the point where they are able to rule out everything else that might possibly be a cause and declare that FASD is the most likely cause. And if they can find evidence of prenatal alcohol use by the mother, that can provide the missing piece of the puzzle.

"That's the tragedy of FASD," says Werner. "Knowing a child has brain damage due to prenatal alcohol exposure can be so

Diagnosing FASD is difficult because facial abnormalities can be overlooked and effects on the brain are not always evident or measurable in a young child.

A Parent Can Tell

In the following excerpt, Kari Fletcher, an adoptive mother of two children with FASD, explains that while her children may not show the typical physical signs of prenatal alcohol exposure, there are other signs that parents of FASD children can see very clearly.

> People may not see FASD when they look at my son's face, but I see it. I see it in the way his eyes flash in anger when he is frustrated and I see it in the tears that pour down his face when he is trying so hard to understand his math problems. I see it in his blank stare when he shuts down after working so hard in school all day, a place that has labeled him as lazy and defiant, and I see it in his silly smile when he is being impulsive or inappropriately friendly with strangers.
>
> FASD is also visible on my face and on the faces of other moms and dads.... It is spelled out in worry lines. For some it is in the tears that flow in overwhelming grief. These are the facial features of FASD that do not appear on the FAS diagrams. FASD is often called the invisible disability, but I see it everywhere I look ... and it doesn't go away just because I close my eyes.

Kari Fletcher. Sidebar at Fetal Alcohol Disorders Society website. www.faslink.org.

helpful early on. It can mean there are more services available for that child. It definitely means that parents and teachers will know that it isn't that a child is 'bad' or 'unruly.' But instead, we see kids in eighth or ninth grade who have just gotten a diagnosis, and by then, we've lost so much time."[35]

No one knows this better than Stephen Neafcy, who was diagnosed with FASD in 1983, at the age of forty-three. "[As a child] I was very slow at learning to crawl and everything was very difficult for me to pick up and learn," he says. "I was still wetting the bed at age 12 and had so many bad habits like biting my nails. I was always confused and never seemed to fit in."[36] After his diagnosis, he wrote of the great relief he felt when he learned his impulsive behavior and school problems were due to prenatal alcohol exposure, which at that time was called "fetal alcohol effects," or FAE. "My problem was not knowing I was FAE until age 43. I was expected to fly with the flock when I had a broken wing! Using this broken wing to try to glide with my peers was a living hell, but the worst was failing and seeing the disappointment in Mom and Dad's eyes."[37]

"She Deserved Better"

But one of the most common difficulties in getting an accurate diagnosis of FAS or FASD is that by the time caregivers and doctors realize there is a problem, the birth mother is no longer in the picture, and her drinking habits during pregnancy are not known. This happens because, if the mother was struggling with alcoholism or could not take care of her child for other reasons, Child Protective Services would place the baby in foster care until the mother is capable of caring for her child. As many as 75 percent of the children in U.S. foster homes have FAS or FASD. In many cases, however, the babies never return to their mothers but are instead put up for adoption.

By the time some of the adoptive parents realize that their child has chronic medical, learning, or psychological issues, and want answers about the cause, it is often difficult or impossible to find the biological mother or another biological relative who may confirm that the birth mother had been drinking alcohol during pregnancy.

"We've got to do better by these children," says Marna, a Minnesota mother whose adopted daughter was not diagnosed with FASD until two days before her sixth birthday. "Olive has several medical issues, including severe asthma. She is also hyper-wakeful, which means she seems to be always awake when she should be sleeping. Besides that, she's had lots of trouble adjusting to any new situation—way, way more than other children her age."[38]

Marna insists that having a diagnosis before adopting Olive would not have changed the decision to adopt her. "Never in a million years would I have chosen *not* to adopt Olive," she says. "She's the light of our lives. But [my husband] Mike and I could have done some reading about the disease, we could have researched it, talked to parents who have children with the same issues. We'd have been more on top of things. Really, we've been forced into a position of playing catch-up since the day we got her. She deserved better than having two parents who were clueless about the biological mother's alcohol use."[39]

Marna stresses that even if the brain damage cannot be reversed, it is crucial for parents and caregivers to find ways to make the lives of children with FAS easier. "[Olive] has struggles, and each day seems to contain one major challenge. My hope for the future is that even if science can't cure FASD, at least we can insist that adoption agencies do a better job getting information to the prospective parents, doctors, daycare workers, and teachers. We'd all do so much better, I think."[40]

CHAPTER THREE

Children Living with FAS and FASD

With the many physical, developmental, and behavioral problems that children with FAS or FASD can have, their biological mothers often struggle as parents. Many of these women are alcoholics, drug users, or live in situations that are chaotic for other reasons. All of these can impact the care of a baby with a variety of special needs. Children with FAS or FASD need the right kind of guidance and home environment to meet these special needs. It helps if caregivers are aware of the child's challenges and can provide a nurturing environment.

"That's What We Feared"

Joyce and David, who adopted their grandson Chase, were well aware of their daughter's alcohol addiction and were certain that she could not raise a child in her current circumstances. As Joyce recalls:

> That's what we feared with Chase. We didn't know right away of the extent of his problems. But it was clear from what the doctors said—brain damage, physical issues likely, behavior stuff—we knew [our daughter] Tina wouldn't be able to handle anything like that. To be honest, she wouldn't have been able to handle even the

easiest baby, one in perfect health. She had no patience, wasn't good at details—and with a newborn you have to be. And she didn't have much interest in trying, anyway. So it was the best thing for Chase to come to us.[41]

Some babies with FAS are not so lucky as to have grandparents ready and willing to raise them. Frequently, in the time between birth and their placement in a foster or adoptive

Many biological mothers of children with FAS are alcoholics or drug users who cannot perform the necessary tasks of raising and feeding an infant.

home, they experience abuse or neglect. If the birth mother is abusing alcohol, she is probably unable to care for herself, let alone a newborn. As a result, the baby could be hungry, cold, or sick without anyone noticing.

Jennifer Poss Taylor learned after adopting one-year-old Ashley that the child had lived in such a chaotic situation. Child Protective Services (CPS) had become involved. CPS workers had picked the baby up from a battered women's shelter and were disturbed by what they found, according to Taylor. "[The baby] was severely malnourished, neglected, and very ill. I was told that when Ashley was picked up, she was sleeping in a stroller on top of soiled diapers. She had a curdled bottle of diluted milk clutched in her delicate hands that she was protecting as if it were her last meal. If [CPS] had not come when they did, it very well could have been her last day."[42]

Mothers Who Realize Their Limits

Sometimes women who are living with addiction to alcohol or drugs will give up their children voluntarily. Julie Williams knows this firsthand. Her adopted son, Brenden, was dropped off at her home by his birth mother, a family friend, when he was eleven weeks old. Prior to that, says Williams, the mother and baby were living in an outdoor storage shed. The mother showed up at Williams's door with her baby, asking Williams to take him for the weekend. She never returned for him.

"He brought his pitiful little luggage, and he moved in with me," recalls Williams. "He had three T-shirts, a pair of pajama bottoms, two diapers, and a bottle. He had never had a bath in his life. He was malnourished and dirty."[43]

She also recalls how difficult he was to care for. Brenden slept only twenty minutes at a time. And when he was awake, he was often upset. Because of the brain damage due to FASD, noises terrified him. Williams kept the telephone unplugged and the television off. Even a flushing toilet would send him into frantic crying fits. And because he hated to be touched, it was almost impossible to calm him down. "If I tried to comfort him by holding him, he'd flail away from me," Williams recalls. "I'd try holding him, rocking him, feeding him. Nothing worked."[44]

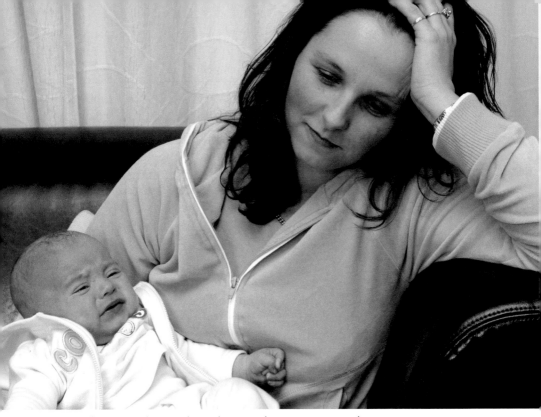

Even the most devoted mothers and caregivers can have a difficult time bonding with a baby with FAS or FASD.

Even the most devoted caregivers can have a difficult time bonding with a baby with FAS or FASD. It can be very frustrating when the child cannot be soothed. Sometimes foster parents will give up on the child and send him or her back to CPS. Worse yet, some will take their frustration out on the baby.

"Fetal Torture Syndrome"

Foster care is usually a safe transition for children who have been removed from their homes, but all too often a child suffering from the debilitating effects of FAS or FASD, receives the brunt of their caregivers frustration—either in the form of neglect or abuse. It is not uncommon, say experts, for a young child to bounce from one foster home to another ten times or more within a year or two.

Dr. Sterling Clarren, whose clinic in Vancouver, British Columbia, sees many children with FAS and FASD, is blunt about the mistreatment those children receive. "After birth they are put into a situation which is high in abuse and neglect. They are taken away from their parents, put into foster care and they are still in an environment of abuse and neglect. Seventy five percent of kids we see in our clinic have seen physical abuse," he says. "We are not seeing Fetal Alcohol Syndrome, folks; we are seeing Fetal Torture Syndrome."[45]

David, a fifteen-year-old boy with FAS, has a brother and sister with prenatal alcohol damage, too. He remembers that he and his siblings were taken from their birth mother when they were younger, but their foster parents were not able to meet the challenge of caring for them. "I went into my first foster home when I was a baby. I was in lots of foster homes because my birth mother could not handle us and did not know how to take care of us. Lots of things happened to us. My brother had three broken arms in one year and I got a big scar on my forehead. All of us were in different foster homes until the last one."[46]

Eva Carner, who adopted a four-year-old boy who later was found to have FAS, says that he, too, was fostered in multiple homes. "He wore out his welcome in a few months wherever he went," she relates, "and had survived at least 13 homes by the time he came to live with me. . . . All of the placements ended because of alleged abuse in the foster home or because Rick was no longer wanted."[47]

Different Sorts of Problems

But even in the most loving and stable of homes, children with FAS or FASD display a range of characteristics or behaviors that are unusual and troubling. Lenore Everett, a Canadian who adopted fifteen-year-old Mack when he was nine months old, was startled at how tiny he was. "Barely ten pounds," she says. "It was pitiful. I wondered if his birth mother had withheld food from him, but that wasn't it. He just had no interest at all in eating or moving around."[48]

She says that she does not believe that even today, Mack feels hunger. "I really don't think he does. When he was little,

The Picture in the Cupboard

Doug and Denise Finnell are the adopted parents of three brothers affected by prenatal alcohol damage. Two, Matthew and Lucas, have FAS, while Anthony has milder alcohol-caused neurological effects. It can be frustrating, they say, because their sons may be able to read a book and tell you about it months afterwards, but they cannot apply what they have read. Discipline is hard, too, because the boys do not understand cause and effect. As a result, rewards and punishments are not successful at all.

As reporters Cara Hetland and Tom Robertson explain, Doug and Denise have a way to deal with the ups and down of raising three boys with prenatal alcohol damage. "When the frustration grows and the boys' behavior is uncontrollable, the Finells open up a cupboard door in their kitchen. Inside, there's a picture of two brain scans. One has normal ridges and valleys, the other is smooth. The smooth brain is the brain of someone exposed to alcohol before birth. That picture reminds the Finnells their children can't help how they behave."

Cara Hetland and Tom Robertson. "It's Like We're Raising Drunk Kids." Minnesota Public Radio. http://minnesota.publicradio.org/display/web/2007/09/05/fasd1/.

we had to make him eat, just little bits every hour or so, to keep nourishment in him. My husband used to say Mack never seemed to notice or care about what we put in front of him, whether it was brussels sprouts or birthday cake."[49]

Everett says that she has since learned that many children with FAS do not feel pain in the same way as other people. "I guess a lot of these kids don't feel the hunger pains," she says. "Some of them don't feel uncomfortable when it's too cold or hot, either. That was Mack, too—he'd walk outside when it was winter, ice and snow all over the ground, and never thought about putting his coat on."[50]

School Problems

Other unusual behaviors are more noticeable when the child begins school. Taylor was aware that her adopted daughter, Ashley, was physically much smaller than other children her age and assumed that Ashley's shyness and fears were a result of her difficult start in life.

But when Ashley began kindergarten, her teacher voiced some concerns that were troubling, says Taylor. "Ashley's teacher pointed out several new, very alarming concerns. Ashley was literally eating a pencil a day. She would gnaw on it until it

Children with FASD are prone to strange behaviors.

was a nub. She would sit on her desk and spin in circles, and she had a very difficult time relating socially to the other kids her age. She would get lost in the halls and tended to fall a lot."[51]

Besides these issues at school, Taylor noticed that when anxious, Ashley had begun to develop some strange behaviors at home. She pulled her hair out and rubbed her hands together, wadding the hair into balls. Sometimes she would eat the hairballs; at other times she would stick them up her nose or into her ears.

Anxious Behavior

There were a variety of triggers for Ashley's anxious behavior at home. Thunderstorms provoked extreme anxiety. Ashley would run to the closet and hide under clothes when a storm warning appeared on television. Sometimes she would become so distraught that she began to pull her own teeth. "The teeth were not even loose, I might add," says Taylor. "She pulled her first four teeth during panic attacks. I asked her if it hurt since they were not even loose, and she gave me the reassurance that 'No, it did not hurt; it just made a weird crunching noise.'"[52]

Taylor says that Ashley, like most people with brain abnormalities, suffers from countless worries and anxieties—both real and imagined. In the car Ashley worries that they might run out of gas or that her father is turning the wrong way to get to where they are going. The family cannot go shopping in the evening, for she is terrified that the store will close. "Once she hears the announcement that the store will be closing in 'five minutes,'" says Taylor, "she starts crying and eventually stops breathing. . . . She can't explain what scares her so badly, but I think she fears we will be locked in the store and cannot get out."[53]

School and FAS

But by far, the biggest source of anxiety and frustration felt by children with FAS and their parents is school. Beginning in the early grades, those with FAS or FASD almost always find it difficult to blend into a social atmosphere with so many rules.

Children with FAS find it difficult to concentrate in class and are often inattentive.

While their parents have become adept at shielding them from loud noises, crowds, and scary situations, school can be all of those things.

For Liz Kulp, a young girl with FASD, the idea of starting school was not frightening. She had had fun in the small preschool she attended, and she enjoyed the crafts, playtime, and stories. Kindergarten was fun for her, too, though there were things she could not do that her classmates could. "While the other children practiced memorization," recalls her mother Jodee, "Liz stared out the window. While the children sang, Liz looked at the floor. While the children wrote alphabets, Liz scribbled. But, she excelled at recess. She made friends with her outrageous personality!"[54]

But by first grade, everything began to go downhill. There was more structure, more emphasis on reading and arithmetic—things that Liz did not understand. Even though she had loved kindergarten, and even though her mother had helped her practice numbers and letters over the summer in preparation for school, she soon realized she could not handle it.

"I felt dumb," Liz remembers. "I asked questions and everybody laughed at me. I always had to sit by the teacher. Everyone could read and I couldn't. The teacher wrote too fast on the board and I could never catch up. I did not want to be there. Kids would tease me."[55]

Jodee recalls that Liz tried to explain to her why she was so discouraged about school. "Mom, it is like every year the teacher talks faster, and faster, and faster, and faster," she said. "I can't hear all the words. I can't remember. I have to make things up. I just answer whatever. I just check off boxes. I don't care if I get the wrong answer. I can't keep up. It makes me crazy. I hate my life."[56]

The Frustration of Schoolwork

As children with FAS or FASD get older, the gap between their ability in school and that of their peers widens. In some larger school districts special programs for children with learning disabilities are in place, and that can help. But in small districts, those options rarely exist.

"For a lot of us, it usually means that you tough it out, working with your child and hoping he or she can get by at school," says Lenore Everett. She continues,

> It's hard, because I know Mack has had difficulties in math and reading since first grade, really. He tries hard, and I think that counts for a lot at his school, because [the teachers] haven't failed him in any classes. But I know that in math he's doing multiplication and stuff he supposedly learned back in third or fourth grade. He gets it and can do okay if you quiz him on it the same day. But in a week, he's forgotten it. And you can't succeed like that in math, because everything builds on the basics.[57]

Ruth Solomon, a teacher from Tucson, Arizona, says such problems are very common with students that have FAS or FASD. Students learn a new skill in math or reading, only to see it evaporate the next day. "Monday they'll be perfect, Tuesday they'll be perfect, and Wednesday they have no idea what you're talking about,"[58] she says, adding that it frustrates their teachers.

The Heartbreak of Being Friendless

One of the hardest aspects of life with FAS or FASD is the difficulty of making and keeping friends. Many FAS or FASD kids are mocked or ridiculed for being slow or for acting out in class when they become frustrated. Even outside of school, they can become frustrated because of their physical limitations.

Liz Kulp loved being active, but her FASD made it very hard for her to do the same kinds of activities her classmates did. "My heart broke watching her struggle to be like her friends—to rollerblade, skate, ski, jump on the trampoline and ride a bike," her mother recalls. "She struggled so hard to overcome her coordination issues and she eventually succeeded keeping hidden for years the hurtful comments she received regarding her clumsiness, inability to skip, her bunny hop, run, and jumping jacks."[59]

Some children with FAS or FASD are so eager to be liked that it is easy for others to mock them or take advantage of them. One Michigan mother says that her daughter, who had full-blown FAS, came home one day, excited that her classmates had voted her the smartest fourth grader, even though she was retarded and took mostly special education classes in her school. It was done as a cruel joke, but fortunately, the little girl did not understand it.

Children with FAS or FASD often find making friends difficult and are the object of other students' teasing and cruel jokes.

Janeen Bohmann recalls that her brother Eric, who has FAS, wanted to be liked so much that he was willing to do anything for a laugh. On the school bus one day, he tried to attract attention by eating a worm. "These attempts to seek acceptance," Bohmann remembers, "only gained him more ridicule and taunting."[60]

Tantrums

Many parents say that episodes of explosive anger and frustration are part of life with fetal alcohol syndrome. That anger comes out of nowhere and often without an apparent cause—making it unnerving for families. Leann Ortman, the adoptive mother of Shelby, remembers how her daughter would frequently erupt into inexplicable rages when she was young. "She raged a number of hours a day," Ortman says. "We're not talking temper tantrums, we're talking restraining hold tantrums. She was completely out of control. It was sad; it was frightening and extremely disruptive. It broke my heart, but when she was done she would just look at me and ask, 'Why do I do that?'"[61]

Nine-year-old Erin was diagnosed with FASD in 2008. She was adopted as a five-year-old by an Iowa family. Her mother, Marta, says that for years anytime Erin became frustrated about something she was not able to do, she would simply throw back her head and scream. "The screaming would go on and on," Marta recalls. She continues:

> It was impossible to even reason with her. We'd talk about whatever it was she'd try to do but couldn't, her dad and I would tell her about things *we ourselves* couldn't do… but nothing helped. The screaming went on and on and on until she was completely hoarse. Erin's screams were so loud, her throat would actually bleed—and I'm not exaggerating. And it would stop just as suddenly. I remember thinking back then I was glad we lived out in the country. If we'd lived in town and had next-door neighbors, they'd have thought she was being murdered. My husband often says that before we had Erin, he would never believe that someone could scream that loud, for that long.[62]

Rage and Violence

Occasionally the sudden frustration and rage of a child with FAS or FASD can produce frightening and dangerous results—too much for even the most loving parents to handle. In some of those cases, the child needs to be in a more institutional setting, with around-the-clock supervision. In her book *Damaged Angels* Bonnie Buxton tells the story of the failed adoption of a little boy named Adam Frank of Alberta, Canada. He was adopted at age two by Lynn and Allen Frank, and at first, the placement seemed ideal. His foster family had mentioned to the Franks that Adam did not often show a temper, but when he did, they should watch out.

At first things went well. Adam seemed to be a sweet, mild-tempered boy. He had an occasional tantrum but nothing severe. When he entered grade school, however, things fell apart quickly. On one occasion, he exploded when he opened his

Children with FAS or FASD can experience frustration and rage, which can produce tension and conflict in the family unit.

Lost

In her book *Forfeiting All Sanity: A Mother's Story of Raising a Child with Fetal Alcohol Syndrome,* Jennifer Poss Taylor explains how her daughter Ashley's short-term memory loss results in her getting lost—even in very familiar places.

> There are times when she cannot even find her way to her own bathroom because she gets confused as to where she is in the house. It is not uncommon to find her walking in closets looking for a common area in the house. . . .
>
> One time, we asked everyone to go get in the car, which was parked in the garage. We got in the car to leave, and Ashley was not in there. We found her in our master closet, which is located on the opposite side of the house through our master bedroom and through our master bathroom. She said she was still looking for the garage. Then another time we went to a birthday party at a friend's house. She had never been there before. She came up to me laughing and said, "Mommy, this house is like our house. I can't find my way anywhere."

Jennifer Poss Taylor. *Forfeiting All Sanity: A Mother's Story of Raising a Child with Fetal Alcohol Syndrome.* Mustang, OK: Tate, 2010, p. 90.

lunch to find a tuna sandwich, which was normally his favorite. Buxton relates:

> He tore the sandwich apart, threw his entire lunch across the room, and then picked up his desk and threw it across the room, while the other children cowered. At this point, Lynn and the school recognized that her son had a serious problem. . . . [On another occasion] he took an exacto knife to school and began waving it around and swearing at people. His father locked up all the knives and scissors

in the house, but Adam managed to find knives anyway, on one occasion slashing everything in the bedroom he shared with his older brother, Jeremy.[63]

Too Much to Handle

Adam had been diagnosed with FAS, and his parents were eager to help him, though his increasingly angry behavior was troubling. Hoping to get more insight on dealing with his outbursts, Lynn confided in a social worker who had a great deal of experience with children trying to cope with FAS. She was shocked when the woman advised her to "pack Adam up, take him to the closest social service office, hand him over, and tell them it's an adoption breakdown."[64]

Lynn, however, was unwilling to give up on Adam. Not long afterwards, the family acquired a nine-week-old puppy. For the first few days, Adam seemed to be happy, and Lynn felt that maybe he had turned a corner and that maybe having a dog to love might help him with his frustration. A few days later, however, she looked out the window and saw that Adam had a large stick and was savagely beating and kicking the puppy.

She rushed outside, grabbed Adam, and asked him what he was doing. Said Lynn, "His reply was the classic FAS 'I don't know.' At that moment I knew in my heart what everyone had been telling me but I didn't want to believe."[65] Several months later, Adam left their family for good, and went to live in an institution.

"Love Isn't Always Enough"

Everett understands that kind of parental helplessness, "I look at my son, and I understand that he's a victim of a cruel disease. He's not naughty or unruly. He's not making decisions to misbehave. It's not like you can punish him and he'll learn not to make that mistake again. It doesn't work that way with FASD."[66]

She stresses that her son's good looks and bright smile used to sometimes make her forget for just a moment that he had FASD.

> He may look like everyone else, and it's easy to think that everything on the inside was like everyone else, too. But it's the wiring inside his brain that's off. That's what they've told us. It's really insidious. It's an invisible thing that makes his brain not work like it's supposed to. I read somewhere that parenting a child with FAS using normal parental instincts is like trying to find your way around Seattle with a map of San Francisco. Boy, I can tell you from experience, that's so true![67]

Marta, the Iowa mother of a child with FAS, agrees. "Those who deal with children with FAS or FASD know that their [children's] confusion and angry frustration is part of their damaged brains, and is not the same as misbehaving. It's not something love and hugs and understanding can cure, any more than you could cure diabetes or blindness or dyslexia that way. It's one of the few times when as a parent you've got to admit that love isn't always enough."[68]

CHAPTER FOUR

Living with FAS Beyond Childhood

The effects of fetal alcohol syndrome, as well as other birth defects on the fetal alcohol spectrum, do not diminish over time. The facial characteristics of full-blown FAS often fade somewhat as a child grows into an adult. But the other problems, such as poor memory, impulsiveness, difficulty with reasoning, inability to make and keep friends, as well as a whole range of learning disabilities, are things that the teen or adult with FAS or FASD will live with his or her entire life.

It Is Forever

Although there are some cases of people with FAS or FASD who can function independently, they are definitely a small minority. Janice Novak, a counselor who has worked with families with children with FAS and FASD, says that parents hold out hope that their children will be able to acquire the skills to be on their own as adults. She relates:

> A mom will say [to me], 'Well, we're doing okay, but *just* okay, with my husband and I both being there 24-7 for our son—and even then there's always a new problem or challenge that comes up.' Then when the child is 17 or 18 and is not a little boy anymore and is getting into adult situations, wanting to be on his own, have a job and make

his own decisions, date—whatever—it's like the parents are in uncharted territory again, with all the issues and problems that come up.[69]

"That's when it really hits them," Novak continues, "that their child, who they've supervised and loved and nurtured his whole life is really not going to be able to handle life on his own. We talk about it, and you gradually can tell that the parents really suspected it all along. But as we all do, we hope that maybe something will just click as these kids grow older. It's just human nature, to hope for the best outcome."[70]

Growing Stronger

Many parents say, however, that when their FAS or FASD children reached their teens, they knew trouble lay ahead. Often it is just the mere fact that they grow physically bigger and stronger that makes a difference in the ability of parents to control them.

Eva Carner is the adoptive mother of Rick, who has FAS. She admits that their life together has been stormy. As a boy

Teenagers afflicted with FAS may have learning disabilities, and find it difficult to control their tempers.

he was destructive and impulsive, two traits that are common in FAS or FASD children. And while she could usually control him when he was little, Rick as a teenager was another matter. By age thirteen, he had grown to be six feet (1.8m) tall and was physically far stronger than Carner.

The breaking point, she says, came when he was enraged and wanted to leave the house, pushing his way past her to the front door. "Simply creating a physical barrier to his bolting no longer worked. He was hardened to physical restraint and more willing to use violence. I could no longer contain him. In desperation, to keep him from hurting others and himself, I grabbed a plastic whiffle bat and tried to keep him at bay by swinging it wildly in front of me. We both ended up with a bloody nose and it was he who called the police."[71]

And Hormones Kick In

Often an FAS or FASD child's growth spurt is accompanied by the onset of puberty. It is very common for these children—especially girls—to experience puberty far earlier than their peers, which means they are often vulnerable to teasing and being preyed upon by older teens and adults. But no matter when the onset of puberty occurs, it brings with it an entirely new range of difficult problems.

Bonnie Buxton, the adoptive mother of a daughter with FASD, asks, "What happens when an alcohol-affected thirteen-year-old has the emotional maturity and academic skills of a child of eight, the sizzling hormones of an adolescent, and, if female, possibly the physical maturity of a twenty-year-old? He or she is likely to become a pariah [outcast] in school just when it seems most important to be popular."[72]

Just as worrisome is the temptation to become pregnant. The idea of having a baby, someone who would love them unconditionally is appealing to some teens with FAS or FASD. "Some think a baby would be a source of affection, somebody to love," says Arizona mental health professional Susan Guinn-Lahm. "But they have not a clue how to take care of a baby."[73]

The Lure of Having a Baby

Many parents try to persuade their FAS or FASD teens and young adults to either be sterilized or use birth control. As one mother relates:

> I had "the talk" with my son. He has a girlfriend, and the last thing either of them should do is have a child. He has agreed that a vasectomy would be the best thing, but I'm not sure he'll actually go through with it. I worry that his girlfriend wants children, and that he'd go along with it. He cannot keep a job for more than a few weeks, and his girlfriend is the same. I'm glad they have each other, but I think I've convinced him that a baby would be a catastrophe for them. And I'm 60 years old, and I don't really want to raise a baby. I know it would eventually come to that.[74]

But many teens and young adults with FAS dream of becoming parents despite their limitations. Twenty-year-old John, who has FAS, has had enormous support from his adoptive mother as he grew up. He knows that he will need help for the rest of his life but worries his mother when he talks longingly about being a father someday. "Don't you think I'd be a great dad, Mom?"[75] he asks her.

She tells him that he would have to take care of someone else and that he has a hard time just taking care of himself. But John fantasizes about himself as a father someday. "It would be neat to have a son to carry on the tradition," he says. "Having a son means you can have man-to-man talks."[76]

One California woman found out that her thirteen-year-old daughter had become sexually active and was worried the girl might become pregnant. She recalls the sad irony of her daughter, childlike in many ways, dealing with a very adult situation. "It was time for [birth control]," she says. "We were at the doctor's office . . . and she wanted to know if she would still get a balloon or sticker."[77]

A Number of Reasons

But the idea of becoming pregnant is only one problem facing young adults with FAS or FASD. One of the most common

Teens suffering from FAS are often impulsive and at a higher risk for early sexuality and pregnancy. Some parents and doctors advocate birth control or sterilization.

reasons that independent living can be so hard is the difficulty in finding and keeping a job. Interestingly, it is not those with FAS who have the most trouble, but rather those with FASD. The reason, say experts, is that many FASD young people do not have the facial abnormalities of FAS and are talkative and often sound bright. As a result, employers often get a false impression of their ability to handle a job.

Ricky, a nineteen-year-old with FASD, is a good example. He moved from his parents' home in Michigan to St. Paul, Minnesota, in 2010. He was hoping to get a job as a busboy or in a fast-food restaurant. He is a good-looking young man and is very talkative; however, he has been fired from five jobs in the past year. He explains:

I have trouble sometimes with jobs. I worked at one place last year. I was answering phones at a [youth] center. It was mostly okay, but sometimes I would get really stressed because I couldn't understand the person on the phone. They'd be talking too soft, or sometimes they'd have an accent that I couldn't really understand. I didn't want to sound stupid asking them to repeat what they said over and over. Sometimes they'd yell at me because they had to repeat who they wanted to talk to. So I quit that job. I just didn't want to go through all the stress. I liked having the money, though.[78]

Ricky is fairly certain that he knows the sort of job he would be best at. "I'm trying to get a job at McDonald's or somewhere like that," he says. "I wouldn't mind cleaning up. I've seen guys out in the parking lot picking up trash people throw out of their cars. I could do that pretty easy. I wouldn't do so good taking people's orders though. I know that, [because] I'd get stressed. Or I'd get mad. But cleaning up, I'm good at that—that would be okay."[79]

Too Stressful

Sidney has the same trouble with stress on the job. Diagnosed with FAS at age fourteen, she graduated from high school and also earned a certificate from a dog-grooming school. She

Young people with FAS often have a difficult time holding a job.

knew a career as a dog groomer would be a good fit for her because she has always loved animals.

She knows now, however, that stress is a part of dog grooming. "Some of these occupations are too fast-paced," she explains. "For example, I worked bathing dogs. That sounds simple, but it's not. You may be working with one animal, but in actuality you are handling many animals at a time. Things come up—the groomer will ask you to answer the phone. Then you have to stop that and do something else—like clean up a mess or do towels."[80]

Eventually, the anxiety Sidney felt at the dog-grooming job proved to be too much. She was not able to explain to her supervisors the difficulty she was having. "My problem was trying to communicate that doing too many things at once was difficult for me," she says. "I don't like asking for help. I ended up quitting abruptly. I wrote a note and said, 'I'm sorry. I can't handle this any more.' They were upset by that. Maybe I need a job that doesn't get paid by the hour but gets paid by the project."[81]

Living on Their Own

There are a number of difficulties with independent living, too. Many parents of FAS and FASD teens and young adults say it has not worked out for one reason or another. "Even with a developmentally normal teenager, life on their own is loaded with potential problems." says Lenore Everett. "But for [my son] Mack, that really wouldn't work. I mean, I can't see it working. Not only would he be responsible for keeping the apartment clean and functioning, but he'd have to do all the things we have to get him to do here at home. I mean, it's everything from taking a shower to getting up on time. And he'd keep wearing the same pants and shirt, and even the same underwear, because he never thinks about changing if left on his own."[82]

For Hunter Sargent, a man with FAS, the main problem of living on his own was his inability to manage money. Because he is considered a disabled adult, Sargent gets a monthly Social Security check to help with his housing. He sometimes spent

When living on their own FAS-disabled people have difficulties performing normal, everyday tasks like vacuuming and housework.

his money on things other than rent, however. "One of the things I've learned, because I'm very, very impulsive—I had some huge nasty bills when I started living on my own," he says. "If I had access to my money, nine times out of ten I'm not going to think about the rent, I'm not going to think about the phone bill. I'm not going to think of electricity."[83]

"I Didn't Know What to Do"

When Bill, a young man with FAS, got his own apartment, he encountered a problem many others with FAS and FASD face. Having not made many friends in his life, he realized that an apartment gave him some status with others his age. Jim Slinn of Parents Resource Network in Alaska writes, "[Bill] hung around the local shelter for runaway or homeless teens and offered others a place to stay as they were about to enter the shelter. Because he had something desirable he felt important, needed, and powerful. Those who came home with him . . . brought him a constant flow of apparent friends, helping to ease his feelings of isolation."[84]

Though Bill did not intend for things to get out of control, they did. These teens began having loud and often disruptive parties. Neighbors complained and called the police. Bill, who was not participating in the parties, was as upset as the neighbors. He did not want to ask the teens to leave, however, because he believed them to be his friends.

When Liz Kulp turned eighteen, she had similar problems. She moved out on her own but says that people took advantage of her. As a result, she ended up being evicted from nine different apartments in a span of two years. "I had basically a party house where friends wouldn't leave," she says. "By me inviting maybe one person, they invite whoever else. But they wouldn't leave and then I didn't know what to do, and eventually got kicked out of apartments."[85]

The External Brain

FAS pioneer Dr. Sterling Clarren has suggested a concept he calls the "external brain" to minimize such problems with housing or finding an appropriate job. He explains to parents that to one degree or another, anyone affected by prenatal alcohol exposure will continue to need guidance beyond childhood. The term *external brain* is actually another person, or group of people, who can do the work of mentoring, guiding, helping, supervising, and supporting the person with FAS or FASD throughout his or her life.

The parents are the external brain for children with FAS or FASD. They provide constant guidance, making sure children get the food, education, exercise, discipline, medical care, and dozens of other things that children need to survive. But as they grow up, people with FAS or FASD want to be independent. They want to have friends, live on their own, and have a job. And whereas their parents would welcome such an outcome, they are fearful that things cannot turn out that way.

Whereas most normal adults learn to successfully monitor themselves, most with FAS or FASD cannot. Because of their brain damage, they have trouble staying on course and often follow impulses that may lead to an addiction to drugs or alcohol. Because they cannot understand the consequences of their actions, they may become victims of crimes, or in some cases, the perpetrators. When children with FAS or FASD grow to become adults, they will continue to need that guidance more than ever.

Teresa Kellerman worries about her adult son John, whom she adopted as a baby. Like many mothers of FAS children, Kellerman has devoted much of her adult life to caring for him. She wonders, however, what will happen in the future when she is not there to monitor him each day. "I look at John, and I think, 'He wants to be independent and he can't be.'. . . It's very depressing."[86]

The Invisible Disability

One frustration faced by many parents with older children that have FAS or FASD is that the extent to which they are disabled is not recognized at all by the public. Society does not see a wheelchair or crutches as they might see with a person who has a spinal injury or muscular dystrophy. They do not see a guide dog or a white cane as they would see with a blind person. Visual cues such as these help the public be more understanding about the difficulties encountered by those with such disabilities.

But because of the lack of such visual cues with those suffering from FAS, says Kellerman, society is less understanding about the problems they face. She observes,

Defining Success

Jan Lutke is a Canadian mother of twenty adopted children, eleven of whom have prenatal alcohol damage. Her story is included in the book *Fantastic Antone Grows Up*. One of her most memorable lessons is that parents like her do not have to accept other people's ideas of what makes for success.

"I define success for each of my children quite differently. Success may mean finishing things some of the time. It means hitting a punching bag instead of a person. Success means knowing who you are, accepting yourself, and understanding that everyone has handicaps. For someone with FAS, success means knowing that these goals are worth striving for, not someone else's unreachable line in the sand."

Quoted in Judith Kleinfeld, ed., with Barbara Morse and Siobhan Wescott. *Fantastic Antone Grows Up: Adolescents and Adults with Fetal Alcohol Syndrome.* Fairbanks: University of Alaska Press, 2000, p. 4.

We would never blame a person who is sight impaired if he were to bump into a table and knock over a vase. We would never blame a person who is hearing impaired if she didn't follow instructions she could not hear. We would never judge a person who could not walk for choosing not to participate in a foot race. Instead we would advocate for these persons to receive the assistive devices needed for them to participate in life in as normal a capacity as reasonably possible.[87]

Such advocacy for those with FAS tends to be limited primarily to the parents of afflicted children. They would like to see a future for their adult children that may include transitional housing, attendants or aides that can serve as external brains, and accessible counseling. But until that can become a reality, there is little help available for those with FAS. As Emily Gunderson of the Minnesota Organization on Fetal

Documentary videographer Margo Manaraze-Wagner interviews an adult afflicted with FAS. Manaraze-Wagner and others like her are attempting to educate the public about FAS.

Alcohol Syndrome (MOFAS) notes, "FAS is really an invisible disease."[88]

The Nightmare Scenario

The fears parents have for their adult children with FAS or FASD are realistic. According to statistics, 80 percent will have difficulty holding a job. A staggering 58 percent of males will spend some time in an institution—either in prison, a mental hospital, or a facility for drug or alcohol abusers. Because of the damage that prenatal alcohol exposure has done to their brains they cannot make good choices for themselves without monitoring from another adult and often behave inappropriately.

That is what Kellerman worries about most. Like many with FAS or FASD, John craves physical contact. Throughout his life, he has loved to give people hugs; however, she says, as he has gotten older, his hugs have become more sexual. She worries that he will get into trouble for inappropriate behavior—something that he does not understand. "We have to have a concrete rule: No hugs," she says. "He can have as many hugs from me as he wants. He has plenty of people providing affection."[89]

But she knows that John is eager to live independently. "I'm going to do what I can to help him reach that goal," she insists. "He has fears about what will happen to him in the future. Maybe we can use this house for John and two or three other people who wish to live here with a live-in person."[90]

Her main goal is to assure that he has supervision. Although she hopes that more help will be available to families struggling with FAS or FASD, Kellerman knows that she cannot count on it. "I've set up a trust fund to pay someone to be a buddy, to come in and make sure he's had a shower or whatever," she says. "I may have to get a job to subsidize his independence."[91]

Redefining Success

Over time, parents learn that their teen and adult children with FAS or FASD will not have the same life goals as those

Fifty-eight percent of male FAS/FASD patients spend time in some sort of confinement, whether prison, a mental hospital, or an alcohol and drug abuse recovery center.

A New Kind of Group Home

In Bemidji, Minnesota, amid green hills and dense forests, is a group home called Westbrook, created for eight men with fetal alcohol syndrome. There is a stable with horses and, along with that, a lot of chores to be done each day. When new residents arrive, they begin living in the main farmhouse, where they are monitored very closely. They do chores each day and learn strategies for taking care of themselves without parental help. They tend the garden and help take care of the horses. Later, when they seem ready to have more independence, they can move to an apartment building on the grounds.

The manager of Westbrook, Travis Dombrovski, is convinced that though life on the farm is often wild and unpredictable, he knows it is better than what usually happens to such men.

"They don't need to be in jail," he says. "Jail is not the right place. Sure, there might be structure, but there's no learning, there's no help, there's no support. And it's a waste of a human life, in my opinion, to leave them in jail. They can come out. They can make it."

Quoted in Tom Robertson. "Adults with Fetal Alcohol Syndrome Face Huge Challenges." Minnesota Public Radio. http://minnesota.publicradio.org/display/web/2007/11/15/adultfasd.

without brain damage. But having prenatal alcohol damage does not mean that success is unreachable. "People talk about redefining success when you're dealing with FAS, and that makes a lot of sense," says Manny, whose twenty-two-year-old son Ramon has FASD. "I know he's not going to be the foreman of the construction crew. But I know he can be a good worker. He can make a good wage, and with help and maybe a lot of reminders, he can even put some of that money in the bank."[92]

Manny says that Ramon has lived on his own for almost three months, although he says it might not be working so well if he and his wife did not live six blocks away. "I don't worry about whether it's going to last," he says. "'It does or it doesn't,' I guess is the way I have to look at it. [My wife] Anna and I are just a few minutes away from his apartment, so we can help out. He comes over sometimes to spend the night if he's anxious about something, and I'm proud of him for doing that."[93]

Manny admits that he has evolved as a father, and it is largely because of his son.

> We didn't know about the alcohol thing when we adopted him. And when we got the diagnosis, it was like a big light bulb went on for us, you know? It explained a lot. And Anna and I were worried about the future—what would it be like for him, how would we handle having a dependent kid when we're in our 50s and 60s? So yeah, the thing about redefining success makes a lot of sense. We heard a doctor speak about FAS once—he said that it's not lower expectations parents need to have. Just different ones.[94]

CHAPTER FIVE

The Latest Research and the Future of FASD

FAS is a lifelong disability that can cause physical, mental, and behavioral problems. From the time FAS was first identified in the early 1970s, and continuing into the twenty-first century, doctors, teachers, scientists, social workers, and parents have been trying to understand fetal alcohol syndrome and the other disabilities often associated with it. Medical researchers are working to uncover more details about how and where in the brain alcohol damage occurs in the hope of better understanding the physiological reasons behind FASD. Teachers and parents are figuring out ways to help those suffering from FASD to cope with their disability and live full lives. Social workers and others are trying to communicate the dangers of alcohol during pregnancy to a wider audience and to help women make better choices.

Brain Studies

A great deal of medical research is focused on finding out as much as possible about how and when FASD develops during a pregnancy. Some researchers are using technology such as magnetic resonance imaging (MRI) to study the brains of children with FASD. From such tools scientists have learned that the brains of people with fetal alcohol damage are smaller and smoother than brains of people without prenatal alcohol damage. But what interests University of Minnesota neuropsychologist Jeffrey Wozniak even more are the differences below the surface of the FASD brain.

Utilizing a technique called diffusion tensor imaging, or DTI, Wozniak uses an MRI machine to zoom in and get a closer look at the brains of children between the ages of ten and seventeen who have FASD. "What we're doing is looking at a milder group of children," Wozniak explains, "who have some abnormalities in terms of their cognitive development, their intellectual development."[95]

The DTI technique, he says, helps him measure the integrity, or effectiveness, of what is called the brain's white matter. "The white matter is like the brain's wiring," Wozniak says.

Some FAS researchers are using magnetic resonance imaging (MRI) to study the brains of children. Shown here is the brain of a healthy three-year-old.

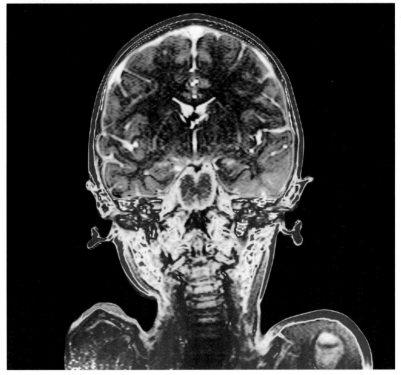

"It connects across long distances in the brain. Its integrity is important because the communication in the brain is at very high speed. Any loss in integrity of the white matter can result in reduced efficiency of the brain."[96]

So, using DTI and other techniques, Wozniak can view the brain at a microscopic level. He says that he and other researchers are learning a great deal about the type of damage prenatal alcohol exposure has done to the brain, which helps them understand why a child with FASD cannot learn or understand things in the same way as other children do. "Thus far, we have learned that one particular part of the brain, the corpus callosum that connects the right and left side of the brain, is affected. This likely contributes to reduced efficiency—slower processing speed—[as well as] more problems with attention."[97]

Diffusion tensor imaging (DTI) allows medical researchers to study the brain's white matter. The brain can be viewed at the microscopic level with DTI and is telling researchers a great deal about FAS.

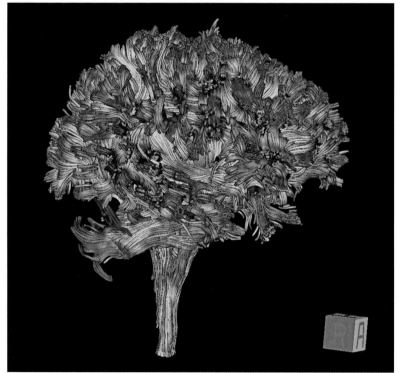

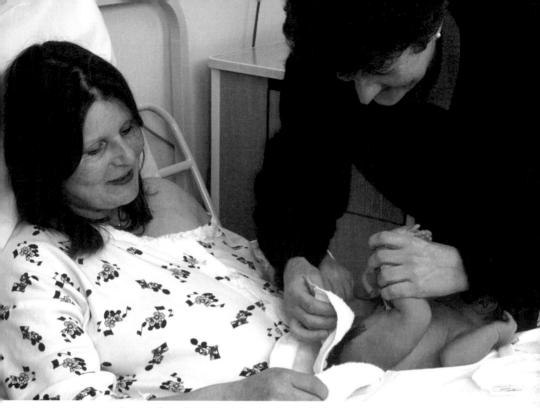

Mothers often lie about how much alcohol they drink during pregnancy. Physicians can easily check a newborn's alcohol level by testing his or her first bowel movement.

Better Diagnosing of FASD

Some of the scientific research has focused on a speedier and more accurate diagnosis of FASD. Many pregnant women who do drink heavily deny it to their doctors, even when their babies show signs of being alcohol affected. "People characteristically underreport the amount of alcohol they drink," agrees Michael Laposata, a Massachusetts laboratory director. "One can measure blood alcohol, but it disappears from the blood relatively quickly after drinking stops, so only very recent [alcohol use] can be documented."[98]

A test developed at the Toronto Hospital for Sick Children, however, can tell doctors very quickly how much alcohol mothers drank during pregnancy by analyzing the baby's meconium, the dark, tarry first bowel movement that all newborns have. The meconium has such a color and texture because before birth, the baby digested fluid in the womb. If there was alcohol in the womb, it will show up with this test.

"Meconium is like a trash can," explains Dr. Julia Klein, director of the laboratory that developed the test. "What the fetus experiences [in the womb] accumulates there, and it stays there until the baby is born, so it's a very good medium for measuring what the fetus is exposed to."[99]

The idea for this test is not to punish the mothers who have drunk alcohol during their pregnancies but to identify the children who are vulnerable and require help. Otherwise, it may mean years of frustration for both the child and the family until the child is diagnosed.

Alcohol and Cell Death

Other research has focused on the specific cells that are damaged by alcohol. Dr. Mary Johnson of the University of Arizona, has been studying Schwann cells, or helper cells found in the brain. "The Schwann cells provide an insulation that helps the nerve impulses to travel much faster," Johnson explains. "These helper cells are important in how the nerve cell attains its normal function."[100]

Johnson and her team have found that alcohol—even in very small amounts—kills Schwann cells. "It's as scary as all get out," she says. "When alcohol was involved, we saw huge decreases in the number of helper cells. The alcohol is killing them. The cell death caught everyone by surprise. These cells are meant to divide. They either go into two cells or they die. Alcohol sends them down the death road instead of the division road."[101]

Interestingly, while many researchers had believed that the most dangerous time to drink was in the first three months of pregnancy, Johnson's work shows that is not the case. "Some of the most complex developmental stages in the brain occur later in pregnancy, and they can be greatly affected by alcohol," she says. "The nervous system is very, very vulnerable in the second and third trimesters [months four through nine of pregnancy]."[102]

Not Only Science

Not all the work being done to understand the damage of FAS happens in laboratories. In fact, some of the most important work happens in classrooms and doctors' offices. Educating the

The Everlasting Guilt

In the following excerpt from "Drunk for Life," the story is told of Debbie Crowell's abuse of alcohol when she was pregnant. She is now ashamed of the consequences of her drinking and says that she shares this information in the hope that other pregnant women will not make the same mistakes.

> With every sip that Debbie Crowell took from the icy can of Budweiser, the tiny baby growing inside her belly became more and more drunk. Crowell, 29, knew that as a pregnant woman, she shouldn't drink. But she had drunk during some of her six pregnancies before this one, and each of those babies looked OK to her.
>
> So she drank. When she got up in the morning, she'd start. When she felt as if she'd had too much beer and was about to pass out, she would use cocaine, so she could drink some more. Sitting in her living room or on the front porch of her Ajo [Arizona] home, she drank until the beer was gone— about an 18-pack every day.
>
> As Crowell got more and more drunk, so did her child, Sabrina, now 7 months old. Doctors believe Sabrina, who started having seizures last month, may have fetal alcohol syndrome. And recently, another of Crowell's children, 3-year-old Cory, was found to have FAS and is brain-damaged for life.
>
> "The guilt is tremendous," said Crowell, who finally found help for her alcoholism this year. "I did it again and again and again. Having to explain that I did that to them is going to be the hardest thing. I don't know how I'm going to tell them. It was something I could have prevented."

FAS Resource Center. "Drunk for Life." www.come-over.to/FAS/Citizen/part1.html.

public—and specifically pregnant women—about the dangers of alcohol to an unborn child is critically important. It is impossible for a baby to be born with FASD if the mother does not drink alcohol during pregnancy. And because some women drink before they realize they are pregnant, it is important to refrain from alcohol even if there is a chance they might be pregnant.

"We've got to get the word out that fetal alcohol syndrome is 100 percent preventable," says Lynnelle, a Florida mother of a six-year-old diagnosed with FASD. "It's the only birth defect that we could completely wipe out right now, if pregnant women would just refuse to drink during the nine months they're carrying their child. That's all it would take, and there would be no more FAS, or FASD."[103]

For years, many doctors have been warning their pregnant patients about the potential dangers of consuming alcohol. But the numbers of children born with alcohol damage show that women are not getting the message. Some FASD experts complain that doctors are sending mixed signals. Denise, a Wisconsin woman who delivered healthy twins in March 2011, says her doctor's stand on drinking was confusing. "I asked him when I first found out I was pregnant about what was okay and what wasn't," she says. "He said if I kept it to one drink a day there was not a problem. He just said no bingeing, which I wouldn't do anyway. But other moms I know were surprised that he said that, because their doctors had been pretty clear about saying, 'No alcohol.' I think expectant moms are really getting two different viewpoints."[104]

Dr. Terry Cullen, a clinical director of Sells Hospital in Arizona, agrees that the medical community is contradicting itself. "As late as 1983, doctors were being trained that drinking is safe in pregnancy," he says. "There are tons of doctors in their 40s and older who are still giving this advice to their patients."[105]

Preventing FAS

Many doctors and other experts are frustrated by the large numbers of children still being born with FASD, even though there has been so much written about the dangers of drinking during pregnancy. Many insist that it is not enough to require

Arizona health officials demonstrate to elementary school teachers what drinking can do to the fetal brain by dropping an egg into a container of grain alcohol. The alcohol begins cooking the egg in seconds.

labels on liquor bottles warning about the possibility of birth defects when a pregnant woman drinks.

What is needed, some say, is a large media blitz. "We've got to make all Americans aware of the serious implications to their children," says Senator John McCain of Arizona. McCain is a member of the board of the National Organization on Fetal Alcohol Syndrome (NOFAS) in Washington, D.C. He believes that the media campaign could be paid for by the taxes collected through the sale of alcohol. "Maybe we need to look at raising taxes on alcohol," he says. "I think there would be a fight [from the liquor lobby], but maybe we could spend some of that money on prevention."[106]

Some, like William Chambless, director of development for NOFAS, thinks new ads against drinking when pregnant need to be more frank. "We have to do with maternal drinking what is being done with smoking. We need everyone in this country to be aware of what happens to these babies."[107]

Pima County, Arizona, juvenile court judge Nanette Warner suggests that such media campaigns might be very successful, as have been the campaigns against drinking and driving among young people. "We used to see a lot of kids drinking and driving, and we see very few now," she says. "I don't know why we don't have big posters [on not drinking alcohol when pregnant] in bathrooms in the bars and everywhere."[108]

"More Labels than a Pickle Jar"

While some efforts are concerned with trying to minimize the numbers of affected babies born each year, others are aimed at improving the quality of life for those who are already living with FASD. One topic that is especially important is education. With increasing numbers of children and teens being diagnosed, it is

More children and teens are diagnosed with FAS every year. For the most part, they are mainstreamed into the educational system.

even more important that they have a place in the school system and that they have learning opportunities that meet their needs.

Hunter Sargent, now a thirty-four-year-old adult with FAS, remembers how difficult school was for him, simply because no one knew what was wrong with him or why he was having trouble in school. "I had more labels than a pickle jar," he says with a smile. "I was mildly mentally retarded; I had attention deficit disorder; I had Down syndrome. I was autistic."[109]

As it turned out, he was none of those things. Not until he was fourteen did Sargent learn that what he had was fetal alcohol syndrome, but by then he had endured many frustrating years in schools that did not know how to teach him. Today, however, some school districts are adapting special programs to the needs of FASD students.

A Different Sort of Education

One such place is District 287 in Minnesota, an area just north of the Twin Cities of Minneapolis and St. Paul. In 2004 the district decided to develop a program that would be tailored to about twelve FAS students with severe behavioral issues. There are usually only four students to a classroom, a plan that makes it less distracting for other students and gives each of them more time with the teacher.

According to reporters Cara Hetland and Tom Robertson, not much academic work gets accomplished. That is because the emphasis is on behavior, rather than meeting traditional academic goals.

"These kids swear a lot," Hetland and Roberton note. "They get violent. It's not unusual for stuff to get broken in the classrooms. Teachers sometimes use video or board games in the classroom, not as rewards, but as tools to keep kids calm. . . . When things get out of control, teachers sometimes use methods that work with autistic kids. They turn the lights down low, they use music or sometimes a light massage."[110]

"We Don't Care About the ABCs"

The reporters noticed that one of the students, a fifteen-year-old named Robert, was calmly playing cribbage with his teacher. They asked him what it was like when he was having a bad day. "Mmmm, you don't want to know," Robert replied. "Those types of days are crazy days. I get mad and start throwing things, and I have to get sent out of the classroom. And then I get even madder and I just start messing up stuff in that classroom."[111]

Teacher Brad Wing says that the program is different because the sort of destructive behavior that is common in his room would not be tolerated in a traditional classroom. But in these classrooms, such things occur as students are learning to recognize the triggers that set off their impulsive behavior.

"We can't punish that [behavior], because it's brain damage," Wing explains. "You would not punish a student with typical mental retardation if they could not learn algebra. So then why

An FAS Child's Best Friend

Some children with FAS have found that a service dog can be as helpful to them as a guide dog is to blind people. When Donnie Winokur and her husband, Harvey, adopted Iyal, they did not know that he had fetal alcohol syndrome. But when he began preschool, they knew something was wrong. He had tantrums, some of them violent. He was diagnosed at age four.

Donnie wondered whether there was a way to help her son deal with his angry, impulsive outbursts and whether a service dog could be trained to help Iyal. The director of 4 Paws for Ability agreed to train a golden retriever named Chancer for Iyal. The boy's tantrums act as the commands for the dog, who immediately nuzzles his neck or puts his paw on Iyal, which has the effect of calming him. When Iyal is jittery and cannot be still, Chancer knows to lay his body across the boy's legs.

The bond between Iyal and Chancer has grown. Iyal is calmer, and he seems more content than before Chancer arrived—and would we expect our students that have behavioral outcomes of their brain damage to be able to control it, when the brain doesn't allow it? We don't care about the ABCs and 123s. You can't learn if you don't have your behavior under control."[112]

Smoothing Out the Rough Edges

A program at a hospital in Toronto, Canada, has a similar goal. Children there are using props and games to cope with feelings of agitation or hyperactivity—two things that can derail school progress.

The program teaches children to think of their brains and bodies as engines. At times, teachers explain to the students, those engines can get too revved up to function properly. To get them to "gear down," the children have a number of options, such as using ear plugs to minimize noises or closing the

that has helped the whole family, Donnie says. "Chancer has softened the hard edges," she says. "We needed another character in the play . . . and that was Chancer."

Some children with FAS benefit from using service dogs to help them cope with the rigors of living with the syndrome.

Quoted in Helena Oliviero. "Service Dog a Calming Presence for Entire Family." *Atlanta Journal-Constitution*, November 6, 2009. www.ajc.com/news/north-fulton/service-dog-a-calming-188966.html.

blinds to darken the room a bit. On the other hand, if they feel unhappy or sleepy, they learn that they should get up and do some physical exercise.

Called the Alert approach, the program stresses the need for children to be proactive. Instead of waiting until they feel frustrated or angry, they can learn to read their bodies and brains before things get out of hand. One mother says it has made a noticeable difference for her ten-year-old son. She says he can lose his temper at even the most trivial things; however, after learning some of the methods of Alert, he can handle things easier. "He is using his strategies, to walk away, ignore it, talk it out," she says. "Sometimes he can step on the brakes."[113]

Hope for the Future

Those who struggle daily with the effects of FASD know firsthand the irony of such a debilitating condition being completely preventable. Eva Carner, whose adult son Rick has FAS, wishes that her generation could be the last to produce babies whose brains are damaged by alcohol.

"Our youth are the next generation of parents," she says, "and we want to create a culture that looks at drinking during pregnancy in the same way that the majority view drinking and driving. It isn't cool and it isn't smart. Think of the disabilities that will not occur in our children and the economic savings to our overburdened medical and social service systems if we lower the incidence of FASD even a few percent[age points]!"[114]

Notes

Introduction: "The World Seems To Move So Fast"

1. Joyce. Telephone interview with the author, April 28, 2011.
2. Joyce. Telephone interview.
3. Joyce. Telephone interview.
4. Joyce. Telephone interview.
5. Joyce. Telephone interview.
6. Joyce. Telephone interview.
7. Joyce. Telephone interview.

Chapter One: The Evolution of a Disease

8. Quoted in FAS Resource Center. "Historical Perspectives." www.come-over.to/FAS/Citizen/part1_4.html.
9. Quoted in FAS Resource Center. "Historical Perspectives."
10. Quoted in Sheila B. Blume. *What You Can Do to Prevent Fetal Alcohol Syndrome.* Minneapolis: Johnson Institute, 1992, p. 5.
11. Ann Streissguth. *Fetal Alcohol Syndrome: A Guide for Families and Communities.* Baltimore: Paul H. Brookes, 1997, p. 3.
12. Janice Parkinson. Telephone interview with the author, July 1, 2011.
13. Darla. Personal interview with the author. Minneapolis, MN, May 21, 2004.
14. Bill. Telephone interview with the author, May 13, 2011.
15. Bill. Telephone interview.
16. Quoted in Tony Jones. "Sterling Clarren Joins *Lateline.*" *Lateline.* Australian Broadcasting Company. www.abc.net.au/lateline/content/2008/s2525239.htm.
17. Quoted in Jones, "Sterling Clarren Joins *Lateline.*"
18. Mary Werner. Telephone interview with the author, March 27, 2011.

19. Quoted in Tom Robertson. "Alcohol Exposure Affects Generations on Indian Reservations." MPR News. Minnesota Public Radio, October 17, 2007. http://minnesota.publicradio.org/display/web/2007/10/17/indianfasd/.
20. Marsha. Telephone interview with the author, April 2, 2011.
21. Marsha. Telephone interview.

Chapter Two: Alcohol's Effects on the Fetus

22. Aisha Charya. Personal interview with the author, Eden Prairie, MN, March 27, 2011.
23. Michael Dorris. *The Broken Chord.* New York: Harper & Row, 1989, p. 147.
24. Quoted in Jones. "Sterling Clarren Joins *Lateline*."
25. Kateanne Ryan. Personal interview with the author. St. Paul, MN, July 1, 2011.
26. Ryan. Personal interview.
27. Sterling Clarren. Keynote address to the Yukon 2002 Prairie Northern Conference on Fetal Alcohol Syndrome. www.come-over.to/FAS/Whitehorse/WhitehorseArticle SC1.htm.
28. Jennifer Poss Taylor. *Forfeiting All Sanity: A Mother's Story of Raising a Child with Fetal Alcohol Syndrome.* Mustang, OK: Tate, 2010, p. 24.
29. Werner. Telephone interview.
30. Clarren. Keynote address.
31. Werner. Telephone interview.
32. M.J. Hofer. Telephone interview with the author, October 15, 2011.
33. Hofer. Telephone interview.
34. Hofer. Telephone interview.
35. Werner. Telephone interview.
36. Stephen Neafcy. "My Life with Fetal Alcohol Effect." www.members.tripod.com/rose62/stephenfas.htm.
37. Quoted in FAS Community Resource Center. "Broken Beaks and Wobbly Wings." www.come-over.to/FAS/birdies .htm.
38. Marna. Personal interview with the author. Minneapolis, MN, June 24, 2008.
39. Marna. Personal interview.
40. Marna. Personal interview.

Chapter Three: Children Living with FAS and FASD

41. Joyce. Telephone interview.
42. Taylor. *Forfeiting All Sanity*, p. 22.
43. Quoted in FAS Resource Center. "Beemer's Permanent Hangover." www.come-over.to/FAS/Citizen/part2_6.html/
44. Quoted in FAS Resource Center. "Beemer's Permanent Hangover."
45. Clarren. Keynote address.
46. David. "Letter from David. 'What I Want People to Know.'" FAS Connections. www.fasdconnections.ca/id33.htm.
47. Eva Carner. "Eva and Rick's Incredible Journey." *Exceptional Parent*, November 2006, p. 63.
48. Lenore Everett. Telephone interview with the author, June 4, 2011.
49. Everett. Telephone interview.
50. Everett. Telephone interview.
51. Taylor. *Forfeiting All Sanity*, p. 42.
52. Taylor. *Forfeiting All Sanity*, p. 76.
53. Taylor. *Forfeiting All Sanity*, p. 76.
54. Liz Kulp and Jodee Kulp. *The Best I Can Be: Living with Fetal Alcohol Syndrome or Effects*. Brooklyn Park, MN: Better Endings New Beginnings, 2000, p. 25.
55. Kulp and Kulp. *The Best I Can Be*, p. 24.
56. Kulp and Kulp. *The Best I Can Be*, p. 29.
57. Everett. Telephone interview.
58. Quoted in FAS Resource Center. "Swiss Cheese Learners." www.come-over.to/FAS/Citizen/part4_12.html.
59. Kulp and Kulp. *The Best I Can Be*, p. 31.
60. Quoted in Judith Kleinfeld, ed., with Barbara Morse and Siobhan Wescott. *Fantastic Antone Grows Up: Adolescents and Adults with Fetal Alcohol Syndrome*. Fairbanks: University of Alaska Press, 2000, p. 129.
61. Quoted in Cara Hetland. "International Adoptions Bring More Alcohol-Exposed Kids to U.S." Minnesota Public Radio, October 2, 2007. http://minnesota.publicradio.org/display/web/2007/10/02/fasadoption/.
62. Marta. Personal interview with the author. St. Peter, MN, May 14, 2011.

63. Quoted in Bonnie Buxton. *Damaged Angels: An Adoptive Mother Discovers the Tragic Toll of Alcoholism in Pregnancy.* New York: Carroll and Graf, 2005, p. 160.
64. Quoted in Buxton. *Damaged Angels*, p. 161.
65. Quoted in Buxton. *Damaged Angels*, p. 161.
66. Everett. Telephone interview.
67. Everett. Telephone interview.
68. Marta. Personal interview.

Chapter Four: Living with FAS Beyond Childhood

69. Janice Novak. Personal interview with the author. Minneapolis, MN, July 6, 2011.
70. Novak. Personal interview.
71. Carner. "Eva and Rick's Incredible Journey," p. 64.
72. Buxton. *Damaged Angels*, p. 175.
73. Quoted in FAS Resource Center. "FAS Victims May Never Have Independent Lives." www.come-over.to/FAS/Citizen/part5.html.
74. Name withheld. Telephone interview with the author, May 22, 2011.
75. Quoted in Gabrielle Fimbes. "A Boy in a Man's Body." www.come-over.to/FAS/boyman/.
76. Quoted in Fimbes. "A Boy in a Man's Body."
77. Quoted in Buxton. *Damaged Angels*, p. 182.
78. Ricky. Personal interview with the author. St. Paul, MN, April 30, 2011.
79. Ricky. Personal interview.
80. Quoted in Kleinfeld. *Fantastic Antone Grows Up*, p. 107.
81. Quoted in Kleinfeld. *Fantastic Antone Grows Up*, p. 107.
82. Everett. Telephone interview.
83. Quoted in Cara Hetland. "Living with FAS as an Adult." Minnesota Public Radio. http://minnesota.publicradio.org/display/web/2007/09/05/fasd3/.
84. Quoted in Kleinfeld. *Fantastic Antone Grows Up*, p. 236.
85. Quoted in Tom Robertson. "Adults with Fetal Alcohol Syndrome Face Huge Challenges." Minnesota Public Radio. http://minnesota.publicradio.org/display/web/2007/11/15/adultfasd/.
86. Quoted in Fimbes. "A Boy in a Man's Body."

87. Teresa Kellerman. "The External Brain." FAS Resource Center. http://come-over.to/FAS/externalbrain.htm.

88. Elizabeth Gunderson. Telephone interview with the author, October 3, 2011.

89. Quoted in Fimbes. "A Boy in a Man's Body."

90. Quoted in Fimbes. "A Boy in a Man's Body."

91. Quoted in Fimbes. "A Boy in a Man's Body."

92. Manny. Personal interview with the author. Brooklyn Park, MN, July 11, 2011.

93. Manny. Personal interview.

94. Manny. Personal interview.

Chapter Five: The Latest Research and the Future of FASD

95. Quoted in Cara Hetland. "New Science on Fetal Alcohol Exposure." Minnesota Public Radio. http://minnesota.publicradio.org/display/web/2007/11/28/fasdscience/.

96. Jeffrey Wozniak, e-mail to the author.

97. Wozniak, e-mail to the author.

98. Quoted in Eurekalert. "Meconium: Baby's First Stool May Provide Clues to Fetal Alcohol Exposure." www.eurekalert.org/pub_releases/2006-06/ace-mbf061806.php.

99. About.com. "New Test Exposes Drinking During Pregnancy." http://alcoholism.about.com/cs/preg/a/aa021110a.htm.

100. Quoted in FAS Resource Center. "Small Amounts of Alcohol Can Hurt." www.come-over.to/FAS/Citizen/part 2_5.html.

101. Quoted in FAS Resource Center. "Small Amounts of Alcohol Can Hurt."

102. Quoted in FAS Resource Center. "Small Amounts of Alcohol Can Hurt."

103. Lynnelle. Telephone interview with the author, May 31, 2011.

104. Denise. Personal interview with the author, Bloomington, MN, June 11, 2011.

105. Quoted in FAS Resource Center. "Messages from Physicians Differ." www.come-over.to/FAS/Citizen/part6_4.html.

106. Quoted in FAS Resource Center. "Many Want Alcohol Tax to Fund Anti-drink Blitz." www.come-over.to/FAS /Citizen/part6.html.

107. Quoted in FAS Resource Center. "Many Want Alcohol Tax to Fund Anti-drink Blitz."

108. Quoted in FAS Resource Center. "Many Want Alcohol Tax to Fund Anti-drink Blitz."

109. Quoted in Gail Rosenblum, "An Inspiring Triumph over Fetal Alcohol Syndrome," *Minneapolis StarTribune*, May 26, 2011, p. B1.

110. Cara Hetland and Tom Robertson. "How to Educate Kids with FASD." Minnesota Public Radio. http://minnesota .publicradio.org/display/web/2007/09/05/fasd4/.

111. Quoted in Hetland and Robertson."How to Educate Kids with FASD."

112. Quoted in Hetland and Robertson. "How to Educate Kids With FASD."

113. Quoted in Anne Mcilroy. "Rewiring Brains Damaged in the Womb by Alcohol." *Globe and Mail* (Toronto), May 28, 2011, p. A8.

114. Carner. "Eva & Rick's Incredible Journey," p. 66.

Glossary

binge drinking: In general, drinking 5 or more drinks for men and 4 or more drinks for women, on a single occasion, generally within about two hours.

fetus: A developing baby still in the womb.

hypothalamus: The part of the brain that controls many of the most basic functions, including hunger, thirst, body temperature, and pain sensation.

MRI: Short for "magnetic resonance imaging"; a complex technique that uses a magnetic field and radio waves to create detailed images of organs in the body, including the brain.

neurological: Having to do with the brain and nervous system.

philtrum: The groove or indentation between the nose and upper lip.

prenatal: Before birth.

teratogen: Any substance that if used by a pregnant woman is potentially damaging to a fetus.

Organizations to Contact

FASD Center for Excellence

Substance Abuse & Mental Health Services
Administration (SAMHSA)
1 Choke Cherry Rd.
Rockville, MD 20857
(866) STOPFAS (786-7327)
www.fasdcenter.samhsa.gov

Part of the U.S. Department of Health and Human Services, SAMHSA is the lead federal agency addressing substance abuse and mental health services. Its mission is to facilitate the development and improvement of prevention, treatment, and care systems for substance abuse and mental health patients by providing national leadership and facilitating collaboration among those in the field.

Fetal Alcohol Disorders Society

2448 Hamilton Rd.
Bright's Grove, ON N0N 1C0
CANADA
(519) 869-8026
www.faslink.org

Formed by parents who were frustrated by the lack of professional knowledge about FASD, this organization is a nonprofit group that serves as a clearinghouse for FASD-related information.

March of Dimes Birth Defects Foundation

1275 Mamaroneck Ave.
White Plains, NY 10605
(914) 428-7100
www.marchofdimes.com
The March of Dimes is one of the oldest U.S. organizations devoted to improving the health of babies. It raises money to help prevent birth defects, including FASD. Its monthly newsletter is called *Miracles.*

National Institute for Alcohol Abuse and Alcoholism (NIAAA)

5635 Fishers Ln., MSC 9304
Bethesda, MD 20892-9304
(301) 443-3860
www.niaaa.nih.gov

The NIAAA, part of the National Institutes of Health, aims at reducing alcohol-related problems by supporting research, as well as by publishing and distributing research findings. Its publications include *Alcohol Alert* and *Alcohol Research and Health.*

National Organization on Fetal Alcohol Syndrome (NOFAS)

1200 Eton Ct. NW, 3rd Fl.
Washington, DC 20007
(202) 785-4585
www.nofas.org

Founded in 1990, NOFAS is a nonprofit organization that strives to eliminate the number-one cause of mental retardation, FAS, by providing educational information on its website and by supporting research on the disease.

For More Information

Books

Bonnie Buxton. *Damaged Angels: An Adoptive Mother Discovers the Tragic Toll of Alcohol in Pregnancy.* New York: Carroll and Graf, 2005. This book chronicles the life of Colette from her adoption to her young adult years and provides side material on the lives of other children with FASD.

Janet Golden. *Message in a Bottle: The Making of Fetal Alcohol Syndrome.* Cambridge, MA: Harvard University Press, 2005. This book contains good information on how FAS was discovered, as well as tackling questions such as "Should pregnant women who drink be jailed?"

Jennifer Poss Taylor. *Forfeiting All Sanity: A Mother's Story of Raising a Child with Fetal Alcohol Syndrome.* Mustang, OK: Tate, 2010. This is an extremely readable memoir of the difficulties, as well as the joys, of raising a baby with FAS that contains very helpful information.

Periodicals

Jill U. Adams. "Alcohol, Coffee, and Baby." *Los Angeles Times*, November 10, 2008.

Mark Cohen. "Vital Signs: There's Hyperactivity . . . and There's Hyperactivity." *Discover*, March 2010.

Independent (London). "Alcohol Damages DNA of Unborn Children Beyond Repair, Says Study," July 7, 2011.

Marguerite Kelly. "Fetal Alcohol Syndrome's Long-Lasting Impression." *Washington Post*, November 7, 2009.

Anne Mcilroy. "Rewiring Brains Damaged in the Womb by Alcohol." *Globe and Mail* (Toronto), May 28, 2011.

Gail Rosenblum. "An Inspiring Triumph over Fetal Alcohol Syndrome," *Minneapolis StarTribune*, May 26, 2011.

Daniel Vance. "Fetal Alcohol Disorder Often Mistaken for Other Ailments." *New Bern (NC) Sun Journal*, February 14, 2010.

Internet Sources

Carla Hetland and Tom Robertson. "Fetal Alcohol Syndrome: The Invisible Disorder." Minnesota Public Radio, September 5, 2007. http://minnesota.publicradio.org/standard/display /project_display.php?proj_identifier=2007/09/05/fasd.

Websites

Centers for Disease Control and Prevention (www.cdc .gov/ncbddd/fasd). This website has a great deal of factual information about pregnancy and alcohol, quizzes and tips about having healthy babies, and brochures and educational materials that can be downloaded or ordered for free.

FASD Lane (www.fasdlane.com). This site is dedicated to articles, stories, poetry, forums, and video presentations about teens and adults with FASD—from the struggles of finding a job to the frustration they feel about their disability.

Iceberg www.fasiceberg.org). For almost twenty years, the Fetal Alcohol Syndrome Information Service published an amazing newsletter. Though it is no longer being published, this site contains many of them, including excellent must-read articles by parents and teachers about the challenges of FASD.

The National Organization on Fetal Alcohol Syndrome (www.nofas.org). This website has information about living with FASD, scientific information about new research, and first-person accounts by parents and children who are living with FASD.

When Rain Hurts (http://whenrainhurts.wordpress.com/cat egory/parenting). This is a website written by Mary Greene, who with her husband decides to adopt two young Russian children, one of whom has FAS. She details her day-to-day struggles and doubts—as well as her insights—about raising a son with FAS.

Index

A
Adolescence, 62–64
Alcohol
  educating women on
    dangers of, 80, 82–84
  effects on fetal brain,
    32–34
  effects on fetus, 32
  effects on nerve cells, 80
  fetal exposure to, 30–31
  first linked with unhealthy
    babies, 10–12
  type of, 24
  use among women aged
    18–44, *23*, *26*
Alcohol-related
  neurodevelopmental
  disorder (ARND), 20, 22
Aristotle, 11, *11*
ARND (alcohol-related
  neurodevelopmental
  disorder), 20, 22

B
Behavior/behavioral
  problems, 51–52, 56–59
  brain development and,
    34–35
Birth defects
  associated with FAS, 17
  substances causing, 28–29
Bohmann, Janeen, 56
Brain

diffusion tensor imaging
  of, *78*
magnetic resonance
  imaging of, *77*
Brain development
  behavioral problems and,
    32–34
Brain imaging studies,
  76–79
Buxton, Bonnie, 57, 63

C
Carner, Eva, 49, 62, 88
Carner, Rick, 62–63
Centers for Disease Control
  and Prevention, 25
Central nervous system
  (CNS), 17
  See also Brain
Chambless, William, 84
Charya, Aisha, 28–29
Clarren, Sterling, 22–24, 32,
  38, 39
Corpus callosum, 78
Crowells, Debbie, 81
Cullen, Terry, 82

D
Damaged Angels (Buxton),
  57
Diagnosis, 36–38, 40–43
  criteria for, 17–19
  research on improving,
    79–80

Picture Credits

About the Author

Gail B. Stewart is the award-winning author of more than 250 books for teens and young adults. She lives in Minneapolis with her husband and has three grown sons.